Protection & Reversal Spells

~

*The Witch's Defense Manual | Powerful Magick
to Banish Negative Energy, Ward Off Harmful
Influences and Embrace Your Power*

© Copyright 2023 by Avril le Roux - All rights reserved.

All rights reserved. No part of this book may be reproduced in any form without permission in writing from the author. Reviewers may quote brief passages in reviews.

While all attempts have been made to verify the information provided in this publication, neither the author nor the publisher assumes any responsibility for errors, omissions, or contrary interpretation of the subject matter herein.

The views expressed in this publication are those of the author alone and should not be taken as expert instruction or commands. The reader is responsible for his or her own actions, as well as his or her own interpretation of the material found within this publication.

Adherence to all applicable laws and regulations, including international, federal, state and local governing professional licensing, business practices, advertising, and all other aspects of doing business in the US, Canada or any other jurisdiction is the sole responsibility of the reader and consumer.

Neither the author nor the publisher assumes any responsibility or liability whatsoever on behalf of the consumer or reader of this material. Any perceived slight of any individual or organization is purely unintentional.

Table of Contents

Introduction 7

Chapter 1 - Magic is Tinged with White 11
    The ABCs of magic! 16

Chapter 2 - A Lesson in Spells 22
    ...What about Wicca? 26
    (Brief) history of spells and magical practices 27
    Lesson number 1 - The basic principles of witchcraft 29
    Lesson number 2 - The psychic forces of a a witch 32

Chapter 3 - Vademecum for Imparting Power to Spells, Formulas, and Potions ... 34
    How to cast a spell and summon magic? 35
    What is the best place to cast spells and manipulate the energies of the Cosmos? 37
    How to access one's inner powers? 39
    How to recognize an evil eye? What is a magical attack, and what are its effects? 41
    01 - Ritual to ward off the evil eye 44
    02 - Ritual for summoning positive spirits to your abode 45
    03 - Ritual to ward off misfortune from your life 46

Chapter 4 - My Grimoire Recipes 48
    The magical tools of the sorcerers 49
    04 - Recipe to promote divination, the ability to predict the future 52
    05 - Recipe for attracting success in business (and beyond) 53
    06 - Recipe for driving away sickness and disease 54

07 - *Recipe to kick-start your creativity* 55

08 - *Recipe for obtaining unexpected money income* 57

09 - *Recipe for saying bye-bye to negative influences that keep you from expressing yourself freely* 59

10 - *Recipe for wishing and wishing you a good journey* 60

Insight - A comprehensive guide to candle colors and aromas of incense burned during rituals 61

Chapter 5 - Amulets 66

The purification ritual for amulets and talismans 67

11 - *Amulet to encourage inspiration (to be commissioned)* 68

12 - *Protective talisman to keep out of trouble (to be commissioned)* 68

13 - *Amulet to find hope inside and outside yourself (to be commissioned)* ... 69

14 - *Talisman for wish fulfillment (using the Ésaüe method)* 69

15 - *Lucky amulet* 70

16 - *Talisman to boost self-esteem and confidence in your abilities* 71

17 - *Healing amulet inspired by the Moon and its cycles* 72

18 - *Friendship talisman* 73

19 - *Amulet to increase chances of a promotion at work* 74

20 - *Talisman for making a good first impression* 75

Chapter 6 - Spells of Forgiveness, Protection, and Reversal 77

21 - *Protective barrier made with salt* 78

22 - *Seal of protection and defense* 79

23 - *Protection Spell with Iron* 80

24 - *Protective mist* 81

25 - *Psychic Defense Wall (Advanced Spell)* 82

26 - Bottled Defense Spell 83

27 - Purification ritual with tarot cards 83

28 - Spell to bless a new automobile 85

29 - Tapestry of Protection 86

30 - Oil of the Warrior Fool 87

Chapter 7 - The Grimoire of Happiness, Well-being, and Success 88

31 - The Mirror of Holistic Wellness 89

32 - The balm that activates joy and psychic strength 90

33 - The seal of charisma and success 91

34 - Making a mela-magic 92

35 - Success rune cookies 93

36 - Magic cover to ensure your protection and safety 94

37 - Restart potion for all the times you feel the need to (re)start from scratch 95

38 - Reversal spell to send his bad intentions back to the sender (Advanced Spell) 96

39 - Spell to soothe the burden of responsibility 97

40 - Potion to attract present and future love vibrations 98

Conclusions 100

Introduction

Before any (educational) journey, it is essential to pack everything you need for a kick-ass adventure. So stow in your *magical* luggage recipes, talismans, filters, and spells with extraordinary powers. In the following pages, I will take you by the hand to discover the *magickal power* that resides within you. Yes, that's right: magic is not an elitist gift reserved for a class of a lucky few sorcerers, far from it. You won't have to ride a whirling broomstick or stand waiting for a letter from *Hogwarts School*, nor will you have to let a talking hat point to your magical household. Instead, magical experience is an art that is learned slowly. It coincides with an iter of rebirth, self-improvement, well-being, and discovery of the *myriad potentials* within you. Just as a *seed* can turn into a centuries-old oak tree to be admired with eyes filled with wonder, so too - if you want to and set your mind to it - you have all the credentials to awaken the magical powers held deep within your soul. Learning the secrets of witchcraft does not mean manipulating others, bending the forces of Nature to your will, or even using magical energy to harm the people around you. Far be it from me to praise the mysteries of dark spells-that set of practices used to cause *pain, sadness, and damaging attacks.* I want to go even further: I make it a point to dismantle *step by step* the prejudices and preconceptions surrounding the world of magical practices, teaching you practically and concretely how to achieve your deepest desires,

realize your full potential, and keep you away from any *evil eye hindering you in family, love, or workplace!*

Becoming a *sorcerer* or *witch* means, first of all, improving your life. Turning it upside down. To discover its secrets. Peeking beyond the veil of customs and habits of daily routine. Accordingly, I advise you to proceed in reading my book if -- and only if -- you are looking forward to walking at a brisk pace along the mysterious path of the Universe. The latter not only brings to light the magic within you but also illuminates the *present and future* destiny that awaits you in the company of the people you love most.

I will never tire of repeating: magic is not a birth vocation. It is a passion to delve into the silent rules of the World and Nature. With the help of the beneficial spells contained in the pages of the book you hold in your hands, you will be able to increase your confidence in your abilities, improve your self-esteem, propitiate good fortune, say *bye-bye to* jinxes and hexes, and also connect intimately and deeply with the people around you.

You can imagine magical heritage as a *universal key* capable of opening all doors. Some locks will be more enigmatic than others, but fear not: go step by step, rely on my method, and learn to recognize the signs of a *genuinely* effective spell or talisman. The only prerequisite for following me on this journey to discover the **magic of protection and reversal** is only one: *yourself.* Dig inside yourself, listen to yourself, and tap into that inner well of intelligence, emotionality, charisma, and curiosity that makes you unique and inimitable. Let yourself be guided by the desire to heal and change the world, starting by working on yourself first.

Now, I can almost imagine the thoughts running through your head, "Ouch, and here I thought I was going to discover who knows what magic formula to use in no time! The way you talk about it, magic sounds more like a psychoanalytic session -- *how boring!*"

Well, you are right. Magic is inseparably related to our psychic and cognitive functions. We cannot separate it from who we are and what we aspire to become. Here is why I put some general theoretical information on paper before recommending talismans and recipes from my very personal Grimoire. I hope they will help you understand the nature of magic and the types of spells you need to become a better witch (or sorcerer), using your talents fully. To succeed, it is appropriate to immerse yourself in our past, in our history. The latter encompasses the birth, mysteries, and riddles of magic used by our ancestors to solve the small-big problems of everyday life.

Curious to know more?

If you are looking forward to learning the ABCs of witches and warlocks, proceed to read with your heart and mind clear of prejudice. Only in this way will you be able to transform into the brightest, most receptive, and most creative version of yourself. It only remains for me to wish you a pleasant stay between the pages of my manual with the words of Paulo Coelho, Brazilian-born writer and author of novels full of enchantment and wisdom: *"Mine is a bridge that allows you to pass from the visible world into the invisible one. And learn the lessons of both worlds."*

Avril le Roux

-Chapter 1-
Magic is Tinged with White

"Everyone must cultivate within himself several qualities that may seem contradictory, such as innocence, self-control, faith, boldness... Activating magic requires courage, purity, and deep work on oneself."

Alejandro Jodorowsky

It aims for *joy*, is animated by *loving* intentions, and increases the *happiness* and *satisfaction* of those who perform and receive it. No, I am not referring to a caress or a relaxing day at a spa. Instead, I am talking about *white magic (or protection magic)*: a cultural heritage somewhere between art and science, between irrationality and logic. Fascinating, mysterious, and dominated by the intuition of those who practice it, it enables cooperation with the forces of nature and cosmic laws to achieve desired effects. Where dark sorcery is a form of magic that intends to harm others or manipulate their minds, white magic (of protection and reversal) fulfills short-term and long-term positive goals.

Yet, the boundaries between good and evil are never clear. Real life is not a soap-opera, fairy tale, or adventure novel with a happy ending. From time to time, the story's hero is likely to turn - into *the antagonist!* Such is the case with an individual who, by serving a spell of falling in love, bends his partner's wishes to his own will. On the surface, love potions are examples of positive magic. They are not. Controlling and influencing emotions represent dark attempts to *"play"* with our interlocutors. In short, do not make the mistake of believing that dark magic is the preserve of demonic forces or large-

scale cataclysms. Wicca shares a stricter view of what is considered "good" and what is considered "evil," advising future sorcerers and would-be witches to ask themselves before each spell, *"What will be the consequences of my spells, and how will they have a positive or negative impact on me and the people around me?"*

My dear reader, I would like to reiterate the importance of *"personal"* before magical work to bring attention back to one of the three laws that every sorcerer absolutely must know: **the law of impression.**

Have you ever heard of them?

If the answer is no, I suggest you pay close attention to the information I will share in the next few pages of the manual you hold. These will enable you to understand why it is *imperative to* act as soon as possible in a positive way toward the social environment and the people we encounter within it.

So, then, what does the law of footprint consist of?

Well, in the past, you have surely felt a significant connection with a smell, a color, or a place. Perhaps because it represents your childhood or a happy moment in your existence, or because, conversely, it awakens in you unpleasant memories and feelings long dormant in your subconscious *(i.e., the "unperceivable" part of the psyche). Suddenly*, a song, a scent, a delicious dish or an illustration, a photograph, a phrase, or an elusive face on the subway activates *something* in your brain. Without almost realizing it, you are invaded by a feeling of well-being or discomfort. The latter causes you to laugh, cry or feel strangely happy or melancholy. In short, *as if by*

magic, any <u>input from the outside world</u> has the (super)power to change your mood in a split second.

The question, then, arises: *why?* Why are there daily micro-experiences capable of making us joyful or of reopening wounds that have not fully healed? The reason is found in the concept of **trace**, of **imprint**. Our psyche overflows with thoughts, memories, and past impressions related to a certain *emotional tone* (joy, anger, astonishment, shame, happiness, loneliness, and so on). Just as the rings engraved on tree trunks enable us to trace the becoming and history of a plant, similarly, fragments of experience also mark us intimately. Writes Eric Pier Sperandio in *The Powers of White Magic*, "There are also intangible and therefore more difficult to grasp imprints. This is because events, people, and places leave imprints on us, which the eye cannot perceive but which our mind registers without really being aware of them."

I guess you are still a little confused.

I ask you to experience the *traces for yourself by* testing yourself. After reading this chapter, lift your gaze from my textbook and observe the space around you. In all likelihood, you are in your abode's nursery, kitchen, or living area. Or perhaps on the subway, in the office, or in a public garden where you love to walk your dog or jog. Perhaps you have spent two, five, ten, or twenty years of your existence within a familiar environment bounded by four walls. Within it, you have collected books and souvenirs from your travels worldwide, as well as childhood memories and gifts, plants, and knick-knacks purchased in the company of a friend or your better half. Each object can call to mind a specific moment of your

past existence, related to the *emotional tone* felt at that juncture. "The places we inhabit are imbued with our life and all that it contains, our moods, our joys, our sorrows, our thoughts; in fact, with everything that constitutes the very essence of being human. We must understand that the traces we leave are imprinted in us from birth and that they increase over the years, according to the events of our existence. We are all responsible for our acts, thoughts, and feelings" *(ibid.)*.

And so, the mystery of white (protective) magic lies precisely in the ability to say *bye-bye to destructive thoughts and feelings to "see the good" within and outside* us. I advise you to set out to seek, cultivate and jealously guard the *positive footprints of the past* hidden in the depths of your psyche. Seek them out and be lulled by their beauty.

In addition, reading this manual will first become the pretext for changing your behavior patterns, interrupting the *loop of sadness, loneliness, melancholy, and negativity* in which you may find yourself at a certain period of existence. The moment you learn to tap into the light energy within you, you will also be able to familiarize yourself with the spells that are the basis of your "career as a sorcerer or witch," respecting the first rule of magic: *the law of imprint*.

Remember: positivity attracts positivity, suffering attracts suffering, selfishness attracts selfishness. Love also attracts love, and this is the path I wish you to travel in the company of your passion and interest in the *magical arts*.

The ABCs of magic!

Protective rites contribute to the heritage of white magic passed down from *generation to generation*. The defensive branch of witchcraft enjoys fame and recognition among "insiders." Protective formulas are frequently used in spells that influence love, healing, money, and (good) fortune.

On the surface, it seems like a contradiction.

After all, the word protection implies the presence of an enemy, obstacle, or threat. Who threatens to disturb our inner or outer world? And most importantly, *why?*

Let me explain.

The second magic rule of a model witch or sorcerer is called the **law of the harvest**. Have you ever heard of *the boomerang effect?* Or the popular proverb "You reap what you sow?" In short, you've probably guessed it: a magician or sorceress's actions have several *consequences*. These depend on the intent, behavior, energy, and goodness of the person casting a spell.

If you hurt, you will be hurt back. If you love, you will be loved back.

Good and evil are not only expressed in the form of *actions* (terrible or merciful). Frequently, influencing our attitudes toward *someone* or *something* are looks, gestures, thoughts, and words. During the hustle and bustle of daily life--a life that, needless to deny it, is more hectic and mentally exhausting than that of our ancestors--we do not have the superpower to be 360-degree aware

of the positive or negative energies within and without us. It may happen to us to hurt our interlocutors without realizing it - that is, completely unconsciously. Consequently, before the *boomerang* effect and the law of the harvest pay us back in the same coin, we have a chance to use rituals and protection formulas to keep ourselves away from *(lesser)* evil.

In short, the evil spells of which we are (often) unwitting victims always have two origins:

A) The result of a *dark spell* cast by evil witches and sorcerers, or

B) Arise from the malice, hatred, and envy generated by us in the past that comes back to visit us after *days, weeks, or years* because of the above-mentioned boomerang effect.

Law Number Two invites us to sow the ripe fruits we will reap soon. Moreover, since we do not have the power to undo past mistakes, we can use spells and protective rituals to master the magical arts while securing ourselves and the individuals we love.

In all likelihood, my words resonate in your mind, like the plot of an animated film or a fantasy novel. Yet, I invite you to reflect on something of fundamental importance: the *world*, *the Universe*, and the inhabitants of *Nature* are united first and foremost by ... *energy!* A "neutral" form of energy that evolves, regenerates, and transforms. Just as the waters of a river, animated by currents, are constantly becoming, the manifestations of Creation also represent an expertly balanced mix of animate and inanimate elements in perpetual *revolution*. Here is revealed why the "*magical and non-magical vibrations*" of life come back *amplified*. Of course, witchcraft

is not meant to delude you: modern magicians know full well that *perfection with a capital P* is not of this world. Still, you always have a little room for improvement to produce positive energies and await the return of *equally beneficial* forces and coincidences.

In other words, protective rituals are the wild card you need to <u>neutralize</u> the enemies, obstacles, hexes, and adversities that await you in the (near or distant) future. *Who can tell?* One thing is certain: you should combine the study of spells with *the personal experience of self-analysis*. The latter will enable you to actively work on the frailties and malevolent weaknesses in your character, in such a way as to minimize the negative energy produced in the present, from this moment forward.

Remember: the acts, thoughts, feelings, advice, vibrations, and gestures we relate to our fellow human beings produce waves of positive or negative energy. The former *will illuminate* our lives like a lighthouse leading lost ships to a safe harbor, while the latter will fill existence with destructive emotions. In this way, the law of the harvest will be fulfilled following the principles governing the manifestations of the Cosmos.

And what about **inversion magic**? If protective rites have the advantage of defending wizards and witches from dark vibrations induced by others or yourself, reversal practices are a <u>hybrid system</u> somewhere between defense and attack. Suppose an evil eye or a negative energy quid should knock on your life's door. In that case, you can use formulas, talismans, and recipes - many of which are contained in the Grimoire you find in the second part of the manual - *to "return to sender" the very unpleasant gift!* As much as reversal

magic is more difficult to master and more complex than protective magic, it has the privilege of intimidating even the most fearsome enemies. It is a 100% working system using which you can recover the balance of mind and body, return to smiling at life, and forget the obstacles that have stood in your way in the shortest possible time.

To succeed and restore peace promptly, you have *four types of sorcery at your disposal*. Of course, the long alchemical and magical tradition provides us with many other *sui generis* protective spells. However, those mentioned above are undoubtedly the systems most used by neophyte sorcerers or those approaching formulas and rituals for the first time.

- **Natural magic involves** the use of stones, candles, and herbs with the intent to govern, release, or channel energy. Not infrequently, it requires monitoring the influences of the Planets, Light, and Sun.

- **Folk magic** is a fascinating and mysterious collection of folk superstitions, ancient practices, and propitiatory formulas passed down from *generation to generation*. Some customs of the past are downright bizarre and baseless. For example, did you know that our forefathers believed they could sell a property faster by burning a statue of St. Joseph upside down in the garden? *If you own a real estate agency, you might as well try, right?*

- **Ceremonial magic** consists of rituals performed with timing, accuracy, and precision. Specifically, the wizard or witch intent on learning the spells in question requires elaborate propitiatory

formulas and ad hoc divination tools. In many books, ceremonial magic is called *"High Magic."*

- **Sympathetic magic** has a very strong evocative value. It is characterized by the performance of symbolic acts related to the intentions pursued by the sorcerer. To succeed, it is appropriate to use everyday objects associated with the goals the practitioner wishes to achieve in the short or long term. We will discuss this in more detail in the next few pages of the manual you hold in your hands.

For the moment, suffice it to know that sympathetic magic is based on the third (and final) behavioral rule of novice witches and wizards. I am referring to the **law of analogy**, in which an individual's vibrations (positive or negative) attract the energies of other living beings sharing the same characteristics. I guess you are still a bit confused. I would like to clarify the concept behind the law of analogy with a very simple example taken from the... *musical world!* Let us focus for a few seconds on *tuning forks of different lengths. The* latter will play different *sound lengths* and will not disturb the sound produced by their *"companions."*

Conversely, if we purchase two perfectly identical tuning forks, we have to play the first one for the second one to start vibrating like its *"twin"--without even touching it*. Human beings are not that dissimilar to the aforementioned tuning forks. We, too, just like these rudimentary musical tuning tools, emit *vibrations at certain frequencies*, attracting living beings who - just like us - "proceed on the same wavelength as us." We do not realize that we are influencing the world, but we cannot refrain from projecting outward the

emotional tones, memories, traumas, love, nostalgia, shame, and the desire to change (for the better) stored deep in our hearts. If we merely emanate waves of despair, negativity, and violence, we will surround ourselves with people and contingent situations that will "duplicate" this nefarious baggage and affect us with unprecedented dark force.

Conversely, if we embrace our creative, joyful, optimistic, and generous components, we will give rise to a climax of positivity, euphoria, and confidence in our abilities. Sympathetic magic is based precisely on duplicating and amplifying the energies within us; activating ourselves symbolically to mimic our successes and desires is the first step we must take to transform ourselves into "positivity magnets" in record time. In the second part of my handbook - the one devoted to the Grimoire and talismans - you will practically understand how to transform my theoretical lucubrations into a tangible reality within everyone's reach.

Let us take one more step forward and familiarize ourselves with the vocabulary and terminology of a full-fledged witch or sorcerer.

How?

Learning the conceptual basis of spells, of course!

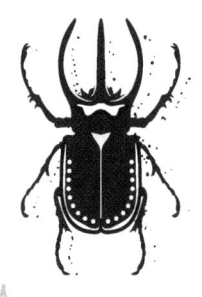

-Chapter 2-
A Lesson in Spells

Your journey of magic discovery has just begun. First, it is appropriate to distinguish between witchcraft and Wicca by reviewing the practical side of a mysterious and fascinating art: *spells*. For, on the one hand, the latter enables the manipulation of energy, which I have already covered extensively in the preceding pages - allowing one to achieve one's goals - and, on the other hand, they guarantee to tap into the powers, talents, and inner abilities of any self-respecting magician. To convince yourself that spells have a tangible result on your life and the lives of the people around you, it is important to keep in mind a golden truth (*Post-Scriptum*: write it down on a post-it note or your agenda as an aspiring sorcerer, because it is the basis of your future success as a novice sorcerer):

Magic is energy that flows within each element of Nature.

And since energy is universal, intangible, and constantly changing, it is also **neutral** (i.e., neither good nor bad). Dark and white magic do not refer to the quality of energy but rather to the sorcerer's use. Witchcraft is, first and foremost, an attempt to manipulate, bend, and twist the course of this energy in such a way as to change its characteristics inside and outside of us. Only then will we at the same time have a chance to enhance our *talents* and *the effectiveness of our spells*.

And don't think my speeches are driven by wacky beliefs contradictory to our contemporary scientific knowledge. It is well-known that living beings are networks (networks) made up of billions of molecules. The bonds between molecules are determined by an energetic potential that, with a little study and practice, can be

modified, (dis)oriented, or channeled in the opposite direction from the original one. The phenomenon I am talking about happens daily in front of our eyes. Have you ever "felt" the presence of an individual or animal behind you without even needing to turn around to check? Or again, have you ever "sensed" the insistent gaze of a stranger as you ride the subway to your workplace on an ordinary rainy Monday morning? Not to mention the coincidences, the forgotten and simultaneously remembered topics of conversation, or that odd occurrence when - after turning your thoughts to a longtime friend - you receive a message from him on Instagram an hour later. How is this possible? Yet, you have not spoken to him/her for days, months, or years!

In most cases, we simply recount these strange incidents with our eyes filled with wonder and share our surprise with other interlocutors. Yet, not everything that happens to us is the result of randomness, far from it. Dominating the above-mentioned phenomena is nothing but (neutral) energy directed outside and inside you.

Spells are *universal tools* to <u>manipulate the force</u> that permeates yourself and the living beings of the Universe. And since energy passes through inanimate matter, it is not surprising that a DOC sorcerer's "toolbox" consists of wood, metals, stones, shells, herbs, and crystals of all sorts. What's more, the exercises underlying the mastery of magic require a mental involvement that closely recalls the meditative practices of the East, Yoga, Tai-Chi, and acupuncture – just to name the "second cousins" of witchcraft.

I would like to reiterate that spells are less bizarre, extravagant, and irrational than is commonly thought. While one should not

consider them a "shortcut" to life's problems, they do not require elite powers. The basis of a spell destined for success is, first and foremost, willpower, faith, dedication, time, patience, and focus on the ultimate goals of the ritual you are about to perform. Even more important is to emphasize the concept that *white magic* is beyond manipulative intent. It will not enable you to win your crush's heart, let alone change the grumpy attitude of a particularly demanding manager or employer. Rather, the task of protective witchcraft lies in the ability to <u>use the energy of the Cosmos to heal the body, empower the spirit, and revitalize positive emotions</u>, which are governed by the law of the imprint I already told you about in the previous chapter.

Before continuing, let me clarify an unfairly underestimated aspect: magic is powerful, implying that the sorcerer takes full responsibility for his or her divinatory interventions. In the role of sorcerer or witch, you will have to commit yourself with dedication and constancy in order **A) not to** break the laws of Nature and **B)** not to afflict other individuals and/or animate beings on Earth with the power of a magical force harnessed in an arbitrary and somewhat chaotic manner. If you choose to purchase the book you hold in your hands and immerse yourself in reading its pages, I imagine you are moved by a sincere interest in the unseen forces that influence the dynamics of the Universe. However, it cannot be ruled out that, among my readers, there are men and women moved by an irrepressible desire to use magical powers to their advantage, heedless of the consequences. But in witchcraft (protection and

reversal), <u>the consequences are often more important than the goals pursued by the sorcerer</u>. Putting personal selfishness aside allows one to achieve improvement not only in the magical art but especially in the exercise of those virtuous qualities - humility, empathy, generosity, listening, positivity, optimism, and forgiveness-that make us *extraordinarily* and *magically* human.

Post-Scriptum: don't forget that <u>energy changes are *always* temporary</u>. There are no rituals or talismans so powerful that they permanently revolutionize the progress of Nature, the seasons, and its *life-death* cycles.

...What about Wicca?

If you have been a magic fan for several years, you will undoubtedly know the difference between Wicca and traditional witchcraft. The above-mentioned magical branches flow into the broader and more heterogeneous category of *paganism*. In any case, not all witches are *Wiccans*, and not all *Wiccans* master witchcraft spells. Adepts of paganism are free to choose which training path to follow: *the secular or religious variant*. What the two pagan approaches have in common is the practitioner's respect for Nature and the laws that dominate the dynamics of the Universe.

Where Wicca is a religious practice oriented toward celebrating certain *natural deities*, witchcraft is characterized by broader and more general practices. As mentioned, the decision to adhere to one or the other "magical order" is up to the adept. Indeed, in both magical systems, <u>it is strictly forbidden to influence or manipulate the will of neophytes</u> by "advertising" one's beliefs. In short, I do not

intend to provide you with overly technical information or niche terminologies beyond my manual's popularizing objective. I want to limit myself to universal advice: keep away from those who, to help you, try to delude you with false promises and rather impose on you to follow the dogmas of a "given belief." Paganism consists of a skillfully balanced mix of experiments, cultural influences, habits, and disparate origins dominated by extraordinary **flexibility.** And it is the latter that transforms magic into a collective good and a *historical-energetic* heritage within reach of all. In other words, I invite you to experience firsthand the benefits of gradually more complex spells so that you can "build" a form of witchcraft tailor-made for you.

(Brief) history of spells and magical practices

Spells are an ancient, indeed a *very ancient*, affair. They have existed since the dawn of history, and they return cyclically in the poems, manuscripts, and essays of the most influential thinkers of antiquity. The Anglo-Saxon term *spell* should be understood in the sense of "motto," "saying," or "tale." And indeed, mastery of **language has** been an essential component of protective magic since Ancient Egypt. Not only did folk narratives passed down orally from generation to generation guard *magical formulas* with regenerative power, but also the bandages intended for embalming mummies were accompanied by the transcription of short hieroglyphic (or *demotic-language*, a kind of *ante litteram* cursive) sayings that were believed to escort the spirit of the deceased king to the Underworld (the Duat).

Witchcraft and its spells experienced *a golden age* until the second half of the fifteenth century - give or take a year. Widespread among Germanic peoples, witchcraft fostered the flowering of *alchemy* and *astrology* and the very first *physical* theories related to the manifestations of Nature and the Cosmos. The term witch comes from the root wik - a word that in the ancient German language takes on the evocative meaning of *"bending"* [energy to the will of the sorcerer]. The first substantial setback to witchcraft occurred in 1486 when a Catholic priest with positions openly opposed to the magical arts gave to print the *Malleus Maleficarum* - from the Latin, "the hammer of witchcraft." The pages of the manuscript called on the faithful to engage in an authentic *witch hunt* considered an unequivocal manifestation of the dark and sinister energy of the Evil One, of Satan. The cleric's theses provoked a *collective hysteria* against medieval sorceresses. It was not until 1542-fifty years after the publication of *Malleus Maleficarum-that it was* established in England by royal decree that magic and witchcraft would be atoned for by the death of the one who dared to contradict the laws of God and the Emperor. One of the most famous events of the past is undoubtedly the grueling *Salem Hearings*, held in Massachusetts and concluded with the sentencing to the gallows of *nineteen innocents* falsely accused of mastering the *"instruments of Satan" in* defiance of existing laws. The persecution of magicians and witches has been a constant through the centuries, demonstrating how magic can both horrify and exert a powerful fascination on the *"uninitiated."* The liberation of paganism from the medieval stigma is a relatively recent affair. In the twentieth century, witch hunts were replaced by

an ever-increasing number of individuals fascinated by spells, magic formulas, and the powers contained in talismans. In the United States of America, at the turn of the 1960s and 1970s, associations, groups, and followers devoted to Wicca or "secular" witchcraft, the difference you have learned about in the previous pages, multiplied by the day. In 1986, in the *Dettmer Vs. In the Landon case, Wicca was finally elevated to a religion by* the Fourth Circuit Court of Appeals members.

However, even though the myriad shades of witchcraft are nowadays considered a *legal* practice and theoretically recognized by society, there are still many (too many) witches and wizards who are terrified at the idea of being persecuted for their *countercultural beliefs*. During my long years of public outreach and magical practice in the public eye, I have had the pleasure of crossing the path of dozens and dozens of "colleagues," who have revealed to me that they rely on the art of witchcraft *in great secrecy, keeping away from prying ears for fear of retaliation with partners, families or work managers who are not very tolerant to the "fantasy corbels of books and novels..."*

Lesson number 1 - The basic principles of witchcraft

My dear reader, my dear reader, in the previous chapters, you have familiarized yourself with the *motion of energy*. However, the three aforementioned rules *(the law of impression, the law of harvest, and the law of analogy)* are not sufficient to guarantee you a magical experience free from complications and mishaps along the

way. In other words, although magic is inside and outside of you, ready to be (re)activated with the power of the spells, recipes, and talismans contained in a *Grimoire*, it is *the intention and goal* you set for yourself during the process that makes the difference. Remember to strictly adhere to the principles transcribed in the next few pages to ensure positive and lasting results.

Caution: do not commit the silliness of believing that the *values of* a novice storyteller are negligible and irrelevant, far from it. They represent the conceptual basis of a magical predisposition geared toward protecting Nature and the magnetic attraction of positive vibrations (within and without you).

Consequently, do not bury your head in the sand or confine your magical art to the practice of spells.

These could turn into destructive tools to the extent that you were to use them arbitrarily, depending on how you get out of bed in the morning.

Yawn, does anyone have a cup of coffee handy?

Let's begin!

CULTIVATE INTUITUALITY AND TRUST YOUR FORCES. As brilliantly established in the law of the harvest and the principle of analogy, the individual energy within you can leave tangible traces on your surroundings. Think about it for a moment: have you ever felt that you were receiving a *message*, *caution*, or *warning* from intuition, that is, from that mysterious and creative force produced by your psyche? Let these little-big mental phenomena flow into your life. Do not keep them on a leash, but open the cage in which

you have locked them up for fear of their *enigmatic and unknown power*. This is the same energy you need to impart intensity and strength to your spells.

DO NOT CONTRAVENE THE COSMIC LAWS OF KARMA. The latter is based on a truth with a capital V: any action performed in the world is returned (with interest) to its rightful owner. Specifically, the Law of Triple Return is an ancient *pagan warning* by which witch-masters warned sorceresses of the past about the dangers of a form of magic subservient to dark, selfish, and manipulative intentions. There are many pagans - including yours truly — who, to this day, live in the strictest adherence to universal karmic principles.

CELEBRATING THE SPONTANEOUS POWER OF SEXUALITY AND REGENERATION. Magic is synonymous with overcoming and breaking taboos. Positive vibrations feed on joy, passion, light, life, contact with Nature and - last but not *least - sexuality* and *sensuality*. Learn to recognize your masculine or feminine component and commit to turning it into an opportunity for *magical evocation*.

UNDERSTANDING THE ALDILY AND ITS SPIRITS *(without fear...)*. Many sorcerers believe in the Afterlife and the phenomenon of reincarnation. In opposition to the notion that time has a *linear progression*, adherents of pagan cults believe that there is an <u>eternal cycle of life and death</u>, interspersed with the experience of *rebirth*. The end and the (new) beginning of the loop are frequently celebrated during the *sabbath of Samhain* when the *intangible, dividing veil* between the world of the living and the dead grows thinner and thinner, almost intangible. And if you think reincarnation is meant for movies, comic books, and TV series, I ask you to suspend judgment

for a while. I hope that reading the following pages, focusing on the driving force of spells, will help you gain clarity.

Lesson number 2 - The psychic forces of a a witch

Where magic is neutral and universal energy, a sorcerer's power corresponds to his or her abilities to channel it into spells, talismans, and saving rituals for self and others. The *power is* not outside, nor is it within the materials, minerals, and magical ingredients you will use as soon as possible. *The power is within you.* As a neophyte sorcerer and novice practitioner, you will likely have difficulty tapping into your *energy chest--without exhausting the energy at your disposal!* The sense of fatigue, mental fog, and emotional chaos that *you may be* suffering from directly on your skin will be **A)** limited *spell by spell* with the enhancement of your powers and **B)** soothed by the help of all those natural energy sources with which to fill your *"magical practice studio."* I am referring to perfumes, little woods, crystals, small animal parts, essential oils, herbs, and ornaments of various kinds. Reducing that all-natural sense of *bewilderment* in the early stages of your study will also be the psychic powers held within you.

CLEAR VISION AND PREVIOUSNESS: The former takes the name "clear vision" or "inner sight" and coincides with the ability to *pierce the veil of the sensible world* to intuit hidden elements or silent presences. At the same time, the latter translates into the ability to foresee events (positive or negative) before their occurrence.

PSYCHOMETRY: The psychic attitude in question allows one to tune into the energy contained in an object or person.

EMPATHY: The latter is an "emotional compass" by which to recognize the feelings and thoughts of others, absorbing their energy.

SENSITIVE ATTITUDE: From time immemorial, psychics have made contact with the spirits of the Beyond to "bring back to Earth" messages from the spirits.

-Chapter 3-

Vademecum for Imparting Power to Spells, Formulas, and Potions

One would think that having understood the study of magical laws, psychic resources, the history of witchcraft, and the values of a budding sorcerer, anyone would be ready to "get down to business" and fill his or her daily routine with white magic, indeed, *as white as snow, summer clouds or sheep's wool.*

(S)fortunately, this is not the case: before even venturing into spells and recipes by which to manipulate the ever-evolving flow of the Cosmos, it is wise to familiarize yourself with the tools and foundations of *divinatory practice.* You need first-hand information to activate the potential within you, formulate *spells with a capital I,* and source auxiliary energies to support your psyche. The following pages are structured in FAQs: an easily searchable list of *questions and answers* to be *read and reread as often as* a *magical* perplexity knocks on your mind's door. Eliminate distractions and noise, pour yourself a glass of wine - or make yourself a steaming cup of coffee, *de gustibus* - and immerse yourself in an enchanting journey of discovery of what you need (or will need in the future) to manipulate the threads of natural energy like Pinocchio's Puppeteer - *but with positive intent, mind you...*

How to cast a spell and summon magic?

That is, where to start to "do something" ...

Everything changes in this mysterious Cosmos where we are born and raised. *Everything flows* - reminiscent of the philosophy of Ancient Greece. In any case, in the shoes of neophytes and budding sorcerers annihilated at the idea of facing the *first* ritual - the first of

many, I wish you with all my heart - it is natural to feel lost, lost and even a little silly, to be honest.

Before you set to work, keep in mind the conceptual basis of a spell. When you perform a spell, you can only take *two paths*: **A)** conjure brand new energy or **B)** manipulate a tot of magic already present in the Universe to change its *course*, its *direction*. In either case, you will have to <u>obligatorily</u> go through the *stage* of *preparing* and *formulating* the ritual. Otherwise, even the hastiest of magicians will behave like a *pentastyle chef* who, eager to serve his diners, lulls himself into the illusion of preparing a dish from his menu without knowing either the ingredients or the quantities or the cooking times. *The result can only be disappointing!*

So, so.

- **Preparing** a spell involves choosing the location, purifying the environment of negative energies, creating the protective circle, activating the magic, and achieving the goal.
- The **formulation** concerns the execution of the spell, which will conclude with the closing of the circle and analysis of the practitioner's achievements.

My dear reader, my dear reader, I would like to point out that *preparation* and *formulation* vary depending on the magical habits of the sorcerer. No "universal dogma" is responsible for the success or failure of spells, talismans, and propitiatory formulas. I employ a <u>permanent altar</u> dedicated exclusively to the practice of my magic. This way, I do not have to purify the environment *before and after* the divinatory experience.

Having established the limits of your *"ideal magical space"* within which you can manipulate the Cosmos flows, remember to draw a **protective circle**. The latter will enable you to keep away negative vibrations and unwanted interruptions from nearby practitioners. To succeed, you can ask a male or female deity for help. Alternatively, *secular* magicians and witches use talismans and objects imbued with white energy. Access the circle of protection and impart strength to the spell using the psychic (inner) and natural (outer) sources friendly to the spell. Many magic enthusiasts resort to talismans, potions, and crystals to increase and sustain their internal energy. Finally, after successfully casting the spell, proceed to "deactivate" the protective circle and cosmic energies that protected you during the practice. This procedure varies depending on the methods you have used to call the chosen deity to you.

The one mentioned above is the process required to cast a spell and summon energy. The procedure is influenced by the practitioner's experience and the magical branch to which he or she belongs. And since you most likely have a thousand other doubts running through your mind, let's not get lost in long theoretical lucubrations and try to understand...

What is the best place to cast spells and manipulate the energies of the Cosmos?

A map for novice wizards and witches

During the long centuries that separate us from the birth of the magical arts, magicians and witches have "trained" their divinatory

powers in various places. Some preferred (and still prefer) to hole up in the four walls of their rooms, and those who rather go into the thick of the woods to get in more intimate contact with Nature and its benevolent influences. Regardless of the *divinatory* environment that piques your curiosity, remember to eliminate the negative influences and vibrations with which it is imbued.

If you have not yet declared your interest in witchcraft, the domestic space is presumably the only one in which you will feel comfortable. *The good news? The* vast majority of spells contained in the pages of the *Grimoire* are performed indoors. On the one hand, the kitchen is the ideal place to prepare concoctions and potions. At the same time, the bathroom is the winning choice should you feel like indulging in a purification immersion or any other energetic ritual in contact with the regenerative element of water.

Practices related to lunar flows, Nature, the seasons, and the passage of time - which for pagans, I remind you, is *circular*, that is, expressible in the form of a rapid process of *birth*, *death*, *and regeneration* - should preferably take place outdoors. You do not need dozens of acres of land to let your *magical verve run wild*. Even a public garden or park allows you to connect with the natural elements and weathering you need to channel your power properly. In short, it's not hard to spot a nook away from prying eyes in which to carry out your *outdoor* witchcraft session. The only universal rule I can share with you concerns the feeling of *safety*, *comfort*, and *well-being* conveyed by the chosen location. There are no dogmas to adhere to as long as you feel comfortable *before*, *during*, *and after* your practice.

How to access one's inner powers?

That is, how to release the magical potential contained within us

If you practice magic occasionally or are unfamiliar with divination, your first concern concerns the ability to ... *awaken your inner power!* In the previous pages, I have revealed a little big *secret for you to keep in* mind: magic is not enclosed in a flying broom or a lucky talisman but within each of us. To activate, awaken and channel it benevolently, you must familiarize yourself with some *propitiatory practices.* You can imagine them as a warm-up that precedes a competitive athlete's performance. To master the energy flows, you should *empty your mind, eliminate distractions, relax your muscles,* and achieve a state of deep *focus* (a deep, enveloping, and unbreakable concentration like the surface of a diamond!).

Many practitioners prefer to prepare for the execution of spells with a short meditation session. Five to ten minutes is enough time to bring your attention back to the vital breath and the emotions, thoughts, and stimuli (input) *inside and outside you. The* preparatory phase is a strictly free and <u>unconditioned </u>magician's or witch's habit. Some prefer to relax by listening to some music and some light scented candles around the house. Essential oils and incense are also good allies to *ward off negativity.* When you have cleared your mind of nagging thoughts and worries, move on to the next steps: **focusing, evoking,** and **stabilizing**.

- **Focusing** allows you to visualize the inner energy flowing within you with your mind's eye. Focus, isolate yourself from outside noise and input and learn to sense the energy *flowing,*

stirring, and *contracting* within you. Strive to follow it, tune into it, and become one with it. *The goal? To* achieve a mental status of balance, peace, and harmony so that positive vibrations can "knock on the door" of your witchcraft session, bringing light and well-being to you and those involved *(willingly or unwillingly)* in the spell.

- **Energy summoning** is a very delicate phase of the whole process. You have no idea how many novice sorcerers make the mistake of *overdoing it*, ending up tired, confused, and drained at the end of a ritual. As mentioned in the previous pages, crystals, and natural objects are valuable allies to preserve your inner magic and enhance the spell's effectiveness. I often use a container of water left overnight under the full Moon. The stratagem mentioned above is charged with a total amount of energy that, when added to that of the practitioner, protects the confidence, strength, and mental clarity of the person about to cast a spell. Or, again, imagine making use of a crystal. To release the potential within, grasp it with your dominant hand and squeeze it between your fingers. Close your eyes and try to visualize the vibrations passing through them. To increase the clarity of your *vision* "color" the energy a blue, yellow, green, scarlet, or rainbow hue. The trick in question will help you activate the chosen object. Gradually, you will begin to feel a warm sensation radiating in the palm of your hand. Do not be frightened, and do not resist. The perception is completely natural. It signifies that you have summoned the magic you need to bring your first spell to fruition. *You are one step closer to manipulating the energy that runs through the Cosmos!*

- **Stabilization is the** last and most important stage. It is done only after pronouncing formulas and rituals, and it helps the sorcerer normalize and rebalance the energy levels messed up by the mystical experience. You can imagine it as being like an electrical grounding. After activating your psychic energy and that contained in talismans and natural allies, you have to dissipate the excess "charge" that has accumulated and...*has now become superfluous!* If you were a novice, consider relying on "earth" minerals and crystals, such as hematite, sodalite, obsidian, and moonstone. Stand upright and bend over so your palms are as close to the floor as possible. The downward-facing physical contact will speed up the outflow of the above energy. Next, close your eyes and focus on your breathing. With each breath, a fragment of magical energy leaves your body and spills out into the atmosphere, air, objects, and living things around you. Surrender to this state of relaxation and deep calm. Then, when you feel you have full control over your psychic resources, return to the chores of daily life and let the effects of your rituals manifest at the appropriate time, following the laws of Nature and the Universe.

How to recognize an evil eye? What is a magical attack, and what are its effects?

Discovering the basics of protection magic

Some believe they are "haunted by bad luck," and those believe they are the (moving) target of a curse. This is not just an ancient superstitious belief but a tool by which *everyone - magicians and*

non-magicians alike - attempts to justify life's roller coaster of ups and downs. I mean, who has never happened to make a superstitious gesture, *perhaps with joking intent?* Who has never "touched iron," dropped salt behind their back, or quickened their pace in the presence of yet another *black cat* running around at night? We are conditioned by a set of irrational, instinctive, and recurring behaviors from which, frequently, we cannot escape.

In particular, the evil eye is believed to be the quintessential *negative vibrations* and *dark forces* hovering around a person (or perhaps ourselves). However, it is worth mentioning that the term in question possesses two distinct meanings: **A)** on the one hand, it refers to a form of curse-that is, a magical activity of a dark nature that the practitioner directs in the direction of another magician/witch in an attempt to bring pain, misfortune and suffering to the unfortunate person. In any case, the evil eye is also **B)** an *amulet* of the most delicate workmanship. In the vast majority of cases, it depicts an *eye*. A millennia-old tradition has it that the talisman acts as an *antidote* to the curse itself. The earliest traces of a *protective eye go* back to the alabaster of Tell Brak, found in Syria and probably carved around 3500 BCE. Centuries later, the German-born alchemist, philosopher, and astrologer Cornelius Agrippa (1486-1535) provided his countrymen with an accurate sketch of the evil eye and its characteristics in the pages of *The Occult Philosophy and The Magic*; the curse thus becomes an expression of a dark force. The negative energy penetrates the victim's gaze and affects his fate and behavior over a period that varies depending on the sorcerer's power. And as the fear of a professionally performed hex spreads throughout the Middle East, Central America, Asia, Africa, and much

of Europe, "laymen" are beginning to wonder about the *signs of a hex*. How to tell if one has been hit by a dark spell (at least according to the version handed down by popular tradition)?

Recurrent symptoms include:

- The victim of the spell lives with a sense of psychophysical malaise, which he or she cannot get rid of, even by resorting to drugs and medicines.
- Severe headaches, fatigue, and mental confusion are the *Three Musketeers* of an evil eye carried out to bring pain and negativity to the affected individual.
- In addition, magical attacks are believed to be responsible for agitation, nausea, vomiting, and nighttime insomnia. The victim's dreams are gloomy and dark.
- Finally, the *typical day* of those targeted by an evil eye is generally punctuated by small or big mishaps; what we commonly refer to as *"misfortunes."*

The main cause of an evil eye and magical attack is the energetic residues of *anger*, *envy*, and *jealousy* nurtured by the perpetrator toward the victim. According to some magical traditions, the negative vibrations encapsulated in a nasty look could also "infect" the interlocutor through a fake compliment, a lie, or a false feeling of admiration related to the successes of *someone* or *something*.

The question begs to be asked: how to keep away from the cauldron of negativity brought by the evil eye, thus finding a way to escape from a *cage of negativity and misfortune* generated by the wickedness and malice of others? Of remedies - as one can easily

imagine - there are thousands. Each sorcerer inclines now for one or another restorative spell, depending on his or her own experience and the (unfortunate) situation of the victim seeking help.

Equally interesting are the *apotropaic rites*, especially in the Mediterranean basin. Some rely on the power of a *talisman, and some make a coral bracelet* or hang a chain of chili peppers outside their front door. Either way, the most recurring amulet in Southern Europe, North Africa, and the Middle East is the *Hand of Fatima*. The latter represents a watchful, wide-open eye painted on the hand's open palm, which is believed to protect the wearer from evil vibrations emitted by dark sorcerers. Some variants repeat the theme of benevolent sight in the *eye of Allah*; the talismans in question are widespread in Turkey and Greece.

01 - *Ritual to ward off the evil eye*

Below, I transcribe the formula I use daily to ward off the evil eye. Use it whenever negativity and bad luck seem to be raging against you, turning your daily routine into an *obstacle course* light years away from well-being, happiness, and harmony.

Ingredients and magic items: thirteen pine needles.

Ritual: After rinsing the pine needles under plenty of running water, chew them for a few minutes. Then, spit them out on your magic and witchcraft workshop floor.

Next, repeat this propitiatory formula three times:

> "I want this evil eye to go away.

Let this spell cease.
Let the evil power return three times in the direction of the black source that generated it.
So be it."

02 - *Ritual for summoning positive spirits to your abode*

Alternatively, if you wish to draw to you the energy contained within the benign spirits - in hopes of thwarting the dark force of the evil eye - test the power and effectiveness of your inner magic with the method below:

Ingredients and magic items: pine or cedar incense, tea seedlings (you can buy them either fresh or already dried), a medium-sized square of yellow fabric, and a candle that is also yellow.

Ritual: After you have achieved a good level of relaxation and harmony in the preparatory stages of the ritual, light the incense and candle. If you have procured tea seedlings that are still fresh, tie them in a small bunch. Conversely, if they were already dried, enclose them in a square of yellow fabric. Finally, bring the tea closer to the candle flame and incense smoke while reciting the benevolent formula transcribed below:

"I call to me the benevolent spirits.
So that they may protect my home
And for everyone to benefit.
So be it."

To reiterate the positive effect of the ritual, I recommend learning about the tea seedlings outside the door of your abode or by the kitchen window.

03 - *Ritual to ward off misfortune from your life*

The last of the three rituals I have been using for a decade now to ward off the evil eye and come to the aid of those who knock daily on my door intending to rid themselves of evil influences. They allow for the restoration of vital harmony one step at a time, eliminating the dark and invisible - but no less disabling - marks of a spell performed by a sorcerer skilled in black magic.

Ingredients and magic items: nine garlic heads, a black-colored candle, sandalwood incense, and a large needle (it should be such that it pierces the garlic cloves. I recommend you prefer models designed for sewing mattresses).

Ritual: *My dear reader, my dear reader, have* you ever woken up in the morning annihilated by an inexplicable feeling of mistrust of your powers and your life? If the answer is yes, experience the effects of one of the most fascinating and powerful *negativity-dispelling* rituals in my *Grimoire*. Light the black candle and burn incense to regain the vitality that flows within you like sap in the branches of a tree. It is best to proceed during the waning cycle of the Moon[1]

---

[1] I advise you to learn more *about the influence of the Moon* and its phases on your spells in order to increase their impact and strength. To summarize, between the two main phases (the Full Moon and the New Moon) there is a transitional period when the area of the satellite *visible from Earth* increases: this is called a **crescent Moon**. Conversely, when the lunar area decreases, we enter the **waning Moon** period. In the former case, the crescent faces to the left, while in the latter it opens to the right. With a little practice, you will be able to turn astrological knowledge into the allies you need to empower and direct its spells in the right way, respecting the laws of the Cosmos and Nature.

when evening falls. Next, get a string and cut it into two sections of about 60 cm each. Thread the twine through the eye of the needle and pierce each of the garlic cloves you have arranged on your purified altar.

While doing so, repeat aloud the formula transcribed below:

"Bad luck, go away.
Get away from me and starve to death
As the time comes
At the end of the Moon cycle.
Bad luck, go away.
That's what I'm ordering you to do."

Speak the invocation in question as you proceed with the addition of all the garlic cloves. Finally, place your *anti-magic* necklace in the room of the house where you spend the most time or which, for whatever reason, you feel is the most important. When you reach the **New Moon** phase[2], bury it in the garden or a park. The bad luck that has been haunting you for a long time will also be permanently *dead and buried* with the help of the protective practices of white magic.

---

[2] The New Moon is the lunar phase in which the "visible face" of the Moon is totally shadowed by the Earth. In ancient times, our ancestors believed that the New Moon was first and foremost the *key moment* of lunar regeneration, that is, the day when the New Moon would illuminate the star-studded night sky. Frequently, in lunar calendars used by magicians and sorcerers, the aforementioned day coincides with the *first of the month*.

-Chapter 4-

My Grimoire Recipes

My *dear reader*, it is time to leaf through the pages of a **Grimoire**: a magical vademecum containing the ingredients, formulas, propitiatory rites, and spells you need to shape the cosmic flow and awaken the dormant magical energy within you.

First, then, let me review some *significant items* that, spell by spell, will become an integral part of your experience. I cannot use my sorceress skills without incense, crystals, mortar and pestle, candles, magic wand, broom, and altar bowl. And since the first part of my spellbook includes liquid potions, allow me to explain to you from A to Z how to source everything you need to get to work.

The magical tools of the sorcerers

You may have guessed it by now: every object of natural origin-if you know how to "activate" and use it-holds within it a fragment of magic and cosmic energy. And since each tool holds its history and inevitable symbolism, passed down through the centuries. *Crystals, formulas, ingredients, and minerals* influence our existence (and that of others) on various levels: love, wealth, family, health, and defense from evil spirits.

There is no doubt: it is now well known that the *modern sorcerer* must develop an open and receptive mindset toward natural energy while respecting universal laws. And since many are the doubts of those who intend to *"train the magical art"* within the limits of their abilities, below you will find a list of subjective reflections on the *must-have* tools that absolutely cannot be missing in any witchcraft workshop:

- The Grimoire - also known as the *Book of* Shadows - all allow the sorcerer to jot down meditations, recipes, spells, and scattered thoughts born of daily practice and/or related to witchcraft sessions carried out during one's "career" - if we can call it that.

- The **altar bowl** will allow you to process different ingredients (herbs, water, crystals, and salt primarily). To get your hands on the model that best suits your magical habits, I suggest you opt for a version with a tall, deep design, preferably made of *natural materials*.

- The **mortar and its pestle** are indispensable allies in aiding the proper execution of *green* spells. They are generally used in the making of bottled or bagged potions but also in the advanced creation of dolls, incense, and candles with distinct therapeutic powers.

- As you may have already guessed about the three aforementioned rituals, candles play a critically important role in ancient and modern witchcraft. They are lit during long-lasting spells or in those that require purification and regeneration of the environment. Generally speaking, a candle with a height of about 20 centimeters will continue to burn for 10-15 hours, while very thin candles (no taller than 30 centimeters) exhaust their flame (and power) in about 9-12 hours. Different colors also correspond to different symbolic meanings. You will understand this better within the pages of my *Beginner's* Grimoire. <u>Warning</u>: I remind you to handle candles with the utmost care. These should always be lit at a proper distance from flammable materials and gases... *to prevent the spell from ending with a bang!*

- **Crystals** are *key - tools* in magic. I like to describe them to the "uninitiated" as *rechargeable* batteries-yes, functioning similar to those in our smartphones and technological devices. Each spell requires minerals and stones of *various make, so it* will be wise to get a **rock crystal** first (among the most versatile and easy to activate). In addition, I again reiterate the importance of purifying your magical items from the energy residue accumulated during the execution of past spells.

- **Incense** is, along with the candle, the wild card you need to decontaminate home environments and your magic and witchcraft workshop. You can choose the variant you prefer: cone, spiral, or stick.

- The **wand of a magician** or witch is undoubtedly the most *stereotypical* tool among those mentioned above. It also takes the name *Athame* and enables the direction and channeling of energy drawn from crystals and natural ingredients in the most friendly and safe manner for the sorcerer and the individuals around him or her. The traditional Athame - also known as The *Witches' Dagger - is* shaped like a knife with a handle covered in fabrics of various colors. Alternatively, the Pointer (the *planchette* Athame) can facilitate the working and personalization of the wand with minerals or crystals with protective powers.

- Finally, the **broom** allows you to symbolically (and otherwise) clean up the neutral space within which you intend to cast a spell or make a potion. It is not necessary to purchase a maxi model; many are the sorcerers (including yours truly) who use a miniature version for dusting tools, ingredients, and the altar.

Equally unavoidable is the use of **essential oils**: liquid essences that encapsulate the symbolic characteristics of the plant from which they are extracted. Since they carry unheard - of potency, you should use them with caution by pouring in no more than 2-3 drops. In addition, it is preferable to dilute them in *water* or a secondary **carrier oil** (such as olive, avocado, or jojoba oil) to dilute their cosmic energies and to bring them closer to the skin in complete safety. Essential oils to add to your pantry as soon as possible so that you are not unprepared when performing long and complex spells include *Bergamot, Rose, Geranium, Cedar, Lavender, Mint, Rosemary, Sage, Sandalwood, Jasmine, Patchouli, and Eucalyptus*.

Let us proceed, then, to discover some *recipes*. Since the capacity of your cauldron may vary depending on the materials and models used, I have not transcribed the exact amount of ingredients. Trust your intuition and evaluate the capacity of the cauldron from time to time. For example, a 250 ml bowl (the equivalent of a glass of water) requires no more than a couple of tablespoons of the *magic mixture* you will prepare in the four walls of your workshop.

04 - *Recipe to promote divination, the ability to predict the future*

Add to your cauldron of water in equal parts:

- **Lavender** (fresh or dried): the plant of love conveys purification, luck, and success. It is generally combined with the two elements of passion and regeneration: *Air and Fire*.

- **Mistletoe** (dried): considered the plant dear to the *druids*, mistletoe is prized by sorcerers of all ranks because of its aphrodisiac properties.

- **Wormwood** (dried): conveys protection, strength, and courage during the ceremony.

- **Marjoram** (fresh or dried): a plant that has always been consecrated to the cult of Aphrodite-the goddess of love belonging to the *mythological pantheon* of Ancient Greece- marjoram propitiates the intelligence, intuition, sensitivity, and gentleness of the sorcerer who approaches the practice of divination.

05 - *Recipe for attracting success in business (and beyond)*

After filling the cauldron with water, add in equal parts a couple of tablespoons of the magic mixture thus apportioned:

- **Basil** (dried or fresh): just like mint and poppy, basil makes it possible to make magic sachets or mix white potions deputed to abundance, fertility, and death. But don't panic: death, in the circular vision of time promoted by pagan worship, is the promise of rebirth and regeneration closely intertwined with the inalienable theme of purification. *After the loudest of thunderstorms and the most tumultuous of storms, the first tentative rays of the Sun always emerge!*

- **Tobacco** (from a cigarette): as much as the (bad) habit of consuming powdered tobacco and herbs was dear to the

sorcerers of antiquity, nowadays, the natural ingredient in question is mixed into potions to **A)** foster communication with a deity and **B)** enhance the effect of oils and minerals. Tobacco acts, therefore, as a *catalyst* and *amplifier* of magical vibrations.

- **Cloves** (whole): employed because of their anti-negativity power, they are very important allies in all those potions and concoctions geared toward annihilating malevolent energies.

- **Carnation** (a pair of flowers): just like the whole carnation, the flowering carnation also allows negative vibrations to be pushed away, promoting the appearance of energy waves intended for prosperity, protection, love, and money.

06 - *Recipe for driving away sickness and disease*

Before procuring the herbs and ingredients from your laboratory pantry, purchase a glass rod. The latter will be turned counterclockwise, with the intent to ward off and disrupt the destructive energies of a disease. The recipe will then be placed in the sick person's room to absorb the deadly vibrations.

In equal parts, add to the water in the cauldron:

- **Juniper berries**: considered to be one of the very first herbs employed by sorceresses in the form of *incense*, juniper protects the wearer from accidents, defends one's dwelling from evil spells, and has the benefit of regenerating harmony and balance lost *before*, *during*, *or after* an illness.

- **Black pepper** (just a pinch): an ingredient that provides protection and banishes negativity from the place where it is poured.

- **St. John's Wort**: According to a *long, long* tradition, St. John's Wort helps ward off the evil spells and curses of sorcerers devoted to dark magic practices. During the Middle Ages, in particular, burning sprigs of the plant in question allowed the Devil to be denied access to a sacred place.

- **Rosemary** (fresh or dried): although used in small doses, rosemary makes it possible to ignite love and passion between two possible partners. In the potion in question, it facilitates the recovery and energy regeneration phase of the sick person.

- **Garlic** (one whole clove): again, garlic is an expression of a natural power that keeps evil influences away (most likely by virtue of its penetrating odor). In addition, it is a remedy prevalently spread against the evil eye, especially in Southern European countries.

- **Cinnamon** (powdered, as well as in sticks): considered a very powerful aphrodisiac, cinnamon makes it possible to win back the heart of an ex-lover but also to return to a phase of balance and harmony that was swept away by a disease or an unforeseen existential obstacle.

07 - *Recipe to kick-start your creativity*

Creativity is a universal psychic predisposition intimately interconnected with intuition and the desire to experience the infinite possibilities contained within *cosmic energies*. After filling your cauldron

with purified water, go on to mix the following ingredients in equal parts:

- 5 ml rosemary
- 5 ml vanilla
- 5 ml juniper
- 5 ml pine needles

Five milliliters generally correspond to one teaspoon.

Take from your pantry also:

- Nutmeg
- Some fresh orange peel.
- A light-blue or silver candle.
- A vanilla incense, which you will arrange along with all the other *green* items on your previously purified countertop.

Ritual: After emptying your mind of daily thoughts, light the candle and burn incense. Wash your hands and fill your magic pot to about ¾ of its capacity. Then, add in order:

- Rosemary, pronouncing the formula, "Rosemary to promote memory."
- Vanilla, saying, "Vanilla activating energy."
- Pine needles, reciting, "Pine for having a thousand ideas."
- Nutmeg, uttering the phrase, "Nutmeg to attract good fortune."
- And orange peel, concluding with, "Orange to improve inventiveness and exercise the intellect."

Remember to bring the mixture to a boil, all the while chanting the nursery rhyme transcribed below (you may vary it if you think you can find terms or synonyms that will facilitate the proper expression of your creative verve):

"Rosemary to aid memory.
Vanilla that activates energy.
Pine needles to get a thousand ideas.
Nutmeg to attract good fortune.
Orange to improve inventiveness and exercise intellect
So be it!"

Before devoting yourself to writing a book, making a painting, or any other activity based on the exercise of creativity and imagination, breathe in deeply the effluvia emitted from the cauldron and allow the inspiration that expands through every pore of your skin to invade you, filling your life with color and magic.

Good luck!

08 - *Recipe for obtaining unexpected money income*

The recipe in question requires waiting for a full Moon night when the Moon is in close proximity to Earth. Generally speaking, the lunar phase calendar reminds us that the full Moon occurs between 14 and 21 days from the time of the new Moon, when the satellite has already traveled one hundred and eighty degrees from its orbit- which is why the Earth ends up finding itself halfway between the Sun and the Moon.

Ingredients and magic items: a green-colored candle, purified water, vétiver incense, 3 bay leaves, 15 ml chamomile, 15 ml mint, 5 ml fennel, 5 ml oregano, 15 ml orange peel. Please note that 15 ml generally corresponds to a tablespoonful, while 5 ml to the capacity of a teaspoonful.

Ritual: Check the lunar calendar and mark the date of the next full Moon in red so that you can prepare the ingredients and proceed with the execution of the recipe. First, light the green-colored candle and burn the vétiver incense until the aroma permeates the four walls of your witchcraft workshop. At this point, fill the cauldron ¾ full of purified water and add the above-mentioned ingredients in the following order:

- First, the laurel leaves, saying aloud the phrase, "Laurel to win."
- Chamomile tea, repeating the formula: "Chamomile to achieve success."
- Fennel, formulating the expression, "Fennel to bless that which is closest to my heart."
- Mint, saying, "Mint to get the right motivation."
- So, the orange peel establishing, "Orange to pocket the money I need."
- Finally, oregano to say out loud, "Oregano to preserve my energy."

Once again, bring the whole mixture to boiling temperature, repeating the ritual aloud in its entirety:

"Laurel to win.
Chamomile tea to achieve success.
Fennel to bless that which is closest to my heart.
Mint to get the right motivation.
Orange to pocket the money I need.
Oregano to preserve my energy."

09 - Recipe for saying bye-bye to negative influences that keep you from expressing yourself freely

It's a well-known fact: wizards and witches are condemned to live with the stigma of a society that stubbornly misrecognizes and denies the liberating power of white witchcraft, protective and never punitive towards Nature and its laws. Consequently, the recipe in question is a must whenever you feel you cannot express yourself freely by sharing with interlocutors "out there" your passion for what you hold most dear: *the art of magic*.

Ingredients and magic items: a white-colored candle, purified water, myrrh incense, 15 ml clover, 15 ml verbena, 15 ml fennel, and 15 ml St. John's Wort.

Ritual: Close the door of your magic and witchcraft workshop behind you, focusing on the feelings of joy and gratitude that invade you every time you take time to cast a spell or get in touch with the magical vibrations contained in the depths of your soul. So, light the candle and burn the incense. Fill the cauldron with purified water to ¾ of its total capacity. Then, add the above-mentioned ingredients one at a time, chanting the magic formula in question:

"Clover and verbena,
St. John's Wort and fennel,
ward off negativity.
Clover and verbena,
St. John's Wort and fennel,
ward off evil
From my residence.
So be it."

Before concluding your witchcraft session, breathe in the effluvia of your potion at the top of your lungs and allow positivity, balance and well-being to reach your body and psyche.

10 - Recipe for wishing and wishing you a good journey

Travel takes on a dual function: it is both a form of adventurous and adrenaline-pumping exploration in distant lands and a chance for renewal and rebirth. Regardless of whether the experience ahead is concrete or metaphorical, proceed with the performance of the ritual transcribed below.

Fill the pot with spring water and add equal parts:

- **Verbena** (dried): verbena serves a self-defensive function. In other words, it provides protection to the sorcerer who attempts to summon and/or summon white spirits to himself.

- **Nutmeg** (grated): testifies to the highest expression of *psychic faculties* and *individual* or collective *health* (all the more so if the concoction is inhaled or drunk by a group of individuals

united by the same travel itinerary). It is a representation of the unbreakable bond that binds companions to one another.

- **Sandalwood** (in shavings or in the form of essential oil): when burned or added to a magical concoction, this ingredient allows one to perceive the presence of *benevolent spirits* (i.e., angelic in nature) in order to facilitate the achievement of *set goals*.

- **Peppermint** (dried): frequently associated with the figure of **Recate**, *the Mother and Lady of all Sorceresses*, peppermint is generally employed in infusions capable of ensuring good luck to the witch or her patrons.

Insight - A comprehensive guide to candle colors and aromas of incense burned during rituals

My dear reader, in witchcraft, every chromatic nuance takes on a different meaning. Symbolism permeates the *"vision of the cosmos"* upheld by paganism and the dozens of machi covens that comprise it.

Below, you will find an easy-to-follow *vade mecum* that you can enrich with your own personal observations and the theories of other sorcerers you will become acquainted with on your journey to discover witchcraft.

- **WHITE**: protection, vitality, regeneration, clarity, and healing from illness.

- **BLACK**: reversal of an evil eye against the principal, protection, termination of a relationship (not just love), estrangement, and forgiveness.

- **RED**: passion, courage, strength, action, and resolve.
- **BROWN**: stability, uncertainty, finding someone or something that has been lost.
- **GRAY**: invisibility, emotional well-being, harmony of body and mind, willingness to compromise.
- **YELLOW**: security, wisdom, recollection, logic, intellectual engagement, and happiness.
- **ORANGE**: creativity, confidence, self-esteem, and an abundance of magical energy within and without.
- **BLUE**: calmness, truth, reliability, security, protection, and, in some cases, depression.
- **GREEN**: money, good fortune, prosperity, and individual and collective growth.
- **GOLD**: wealth and social recognition.
- **SILVER**: goals, mental awakening, vision, and improvement of psychic abilities of the sorcerer.
- **PINK**: love, romance, friendship, honor, and attraction of opposites.
- **VIOLET**: talent, divination, recollection, dreams, and the ability to enhance psychic and magical performance.

In addition, the power contained in the colors is mixed with that conveyed by **litanies, chants and formulas**. You can recite the rituals transcribed in the pages of my personal *Grimoire* or compose the spells you deem appropriate to convey and direct the positive vibrations induced by your white witchcraft.

A very special correlation is that which links incense burned in the course of divination practice to the **elements of nature**. Below you will find an illustrative table.

Again, feel free to jot down in your magic notebook observations and information gleaned as much from direct practice as from sharing knowledge with other novice (and other) sorcerers.

After all, as I see it, the beauty of the magical arts lies precisely in this: in the possibility of enriching, enhancing, and personalizing one's "witchcraft training" sessions within the four walls of a workshop in such a way as to make the divination practice unique and original.

- **EARTH**: All incenses containing plant particles influenced by the earth allow for increased protection, achievement of balance, peace, fertility, achievement of success, and improvement of the financial situations of the sorcerer or his patrons. Some of the most popular incenses include fern, magnolia, mallow, honeysuckle, narcissus, rhubarb, verbena, vétiver, patchouli, oakmoss, and tulip tree.

- **FIRE**: The natural element in question contributes to the enhancement of psychic powers. Wizards and witches may burn fire incense to also increase courage, responsiveness, passion, creativity, and the desire to experiment. Popular plants include angelica, orange, coffee, cinnamon, cedar, garlic, copal, coriander, Jamaica pepper, rose-geranium, dragon's blood, tobacco, tangerine, nutmeg, olibanum, juniper, fennel, ginger, and lime.

- **AIR**: Incenses made from air-protected plants promote communication with positive spirits, keep travelers and explorers

safe, increase powers of divination (i.e., those that enable the sorcerer to predict the course of the future), and ensure physical, psychic, and emotional freedom. Among the most popular incenses in magician's workshops around the world are benzoin, bergamot, lemon, marjoram, fennel, lavender, mint, lily of the valley, sage, parsley, verbena, anise, acacia, gum arabic, and mastic gum.

- **WATER**: Incenses in your pantry that contain one or more plants with aquatic influence help speed the healing of the sick, bring harmony and reconciliation in the family, increase friendship and trust in others, and also promote listening, compassion, and forgiveness. In addition, the *green* products transcribed below have the advantage of making the premonitory dreams that knock on the sorcerer's "door of consciousness" during the night hours more vivid and easily memorized. Among the most popular incenses used in modern witchcraft are orchid, peach, pear, rose, thyme, vanilla, violet, cherry, catnip, heather, chamomile, lotus, lilac, myrrh, thyme, hyacinth, and ylang ylang.

The spells and rituals practiced during your long career as a sorcerer, moreover, should take into account both the **phases of the** Moon - which you can study by consulting a special calendar - as well as the cyclical progression of the **seasons.** By using a plant or part of a plant during the corresponding season, you can ensure longer-lasting and more efficient results in the short and long term. Remember: magic promotes a return to Nature and its slow rhythms. The magician's or witch's momentary wish may not always be fulfilled at the exact instant it manifests. It is best to wait for the

right times and conditions to operate within the laws that uphold the Cosmos and its inhabitants.

- **SUMMER**: Spicy flowers, ginger, and carnation.
- **WINTER**: rosemary, pine, olibanum, and all incense with a strong resinous odor.
- **SPRING**: the rose, jasmine, and all the flowers that bloom with the first warm weather.
- **AUTUMN**: patchouli, vétiver, oak moss, and all the above-mentioned earthy incense.

A further form of *cosmic correspondence* exists between the plants (and their incenses) and the days of the week most suitable for performing a given propitiatory ritual:

MONDAY: lemon, sandalwood, and jasmine.

TUESDAY: coriander, ginger, narcissus, and basil.

WEDNESDAY: lavender, sage, eucalyptus, and benzoin.

THURSDAY: clove, oakmoss, and limousine.

FRIDAY: Rose and cardamom.

SATURDAY: mimosa, myrrh, cypress, and patchouli.

SUNDAY: rosemary, cedar, and olibanum.

-Chapter 5-
Amulets

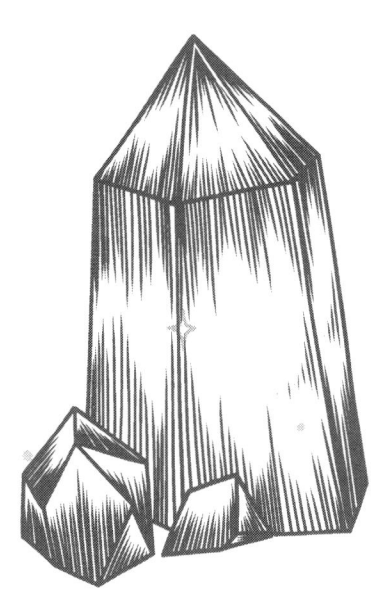

Talismans and amulets imbued with *white energy* are indispensable tools for sorcerers seeking their calling. They are not difficult to make, as long as the aspiring magician remembers to consecrate them before their use. In other words, before wearing an amulet made following the directions in my *Grimoire* or those in any other master sorcerer's magic book, remember to proceed with the purification ritual I have transcribed below. Otherwise, the positive vibrations of the talisman will be irreparably compromised.

The purification ritual for amulets and talismans

Obtain from your workshop pantry some olibanum incense. Burn it and let the talisman swing through the swirls of smoke that hover in the air, left and right - with an almost hypnotic rhythm. While doing so, eliminate distractions and focus the words of this magic formula in your mind:

"*Omnipresent Mother Earth, give me the grace to receive the forces you inspire.
I beg you, in the name of all the goddesses and the gods of your Parthenon, to grant me the fulfillment of my requests.
Mother Earth, bounty of all graces.
So be it!*"

The ritual in question comes in many variations, depending on the goals you intend to pursue with the help of your talisman. Feel free to modify the invocation formula so that you can feel its strength,

vitality, and purifying energy within and without as the volutes of olibanum incense fill your lungs and drive away evil forces from your mind.

11 - *Amulet to encourage inspiration* (to be commissioned)

Sorcerers intent on awakening their creativity through one (or more) Inspiring Muses should commission the carving of a snake. The animal will be coiled all around a Sun with radiant rays deployed in a radiant manner. Wear the jewel hanging around your neck, preferably serving a silver or topaz metal base. In the event that you wish to rely on the power of the amulet *even before* its engraving, draw the reptile on a sheet of your magic notebook and invoke its protection as often as you feel you lack the insight and imagination you need to carry out your daily magical practice.

12 - *Protective talisman to keep out of trouble* (to be commissioned)

What I recommend you carry with you at all times is an amulet to wear before a trip by air, sea, or land or at an important professional meeting that could change your life (for the better). Get a metal plate of the material you prefer and commission the engraving of the phrase, "*Quickly and safely with Mother Earth.*"

13 - *Amulet to find hope inside and outside yourself* (to be commissioned)

In ancient times, the symbol of hope was exemplified in a cluster of olives. You could engrave it on a sheet of copper or gold, wearing it around your neck or in your pocket as if it were a locket. With the help of the protective magic enclosed within your sorcery, you will never lose hope in times of trouble. In short, is it not true that the *sorcerer with a capital F* is the one who, first and foremost, faces the forces of evil by relying on the cosmic rules that uphold Nature and the Universe?

14 - *Talisman for wish fulfillment (using the Ésaüe method)*

Raise your hand if you do not keep a dream in your drawer, hoping to fulfill it under the sign of *good fortune* and *protection magic*. However, the ritual that I recommend you transcribe into your *Grimoire* has a reduced effectiveness: you will be able to ask the magic contained in the phenomena of Nature for the realization of <u>only one wish at a time</u>. To succeed, commit yourself to summoning the *magic square* named **Ésaüe**. After drawing a few drops of blood from the palm of your left hand, take up the pen with your right (your dominant hand) and write the following letters on a sheet of parchment:

ESAU

SAUE

AUES
UESA

Carry the *talisman paper* with you until the complete fulfillment of the wish on which you have poured your positive psychic energies.

15 - *Lucky amulet*

The lucky charm amulet is inspired by the **Fehu** rune of good fortune, wealth, and a thousand opportunities. I advise you to perform it without further delay if you are in the throes of a period of your existence in which the lack of new horizons seems to have a crippling and negative impact on your magical (and other) experience. In addition, I recommend that you proceed with the ritual performance on a *Thursday* or, better yet, *during a Crescent Moon*.

Ingredients and magic items: a small round-shaped piece of wood (preferably 5-7 centimeters in diameter), sandpaper, and a knife. Alternatively, you can also use a permanent marker.

Ritual: After cleansing the altar of energies enclosed in your magic and sorcery workshop, run sandpaper over the wooden surface to smooth the edges and the area where you will proceed with the carving. Then, with your knife or marker, reproduce the Fehu rune symbol on the wood. Meanwhile, repeat the formula out loud:

"Fehu, rune of good fortune, favor my undertakings, bring me good luck and new beginnings."

16 - Talisman to boost self-esteem and confidence in your abilities

Sorcerers everywhere know the feeling of frustration, demotivation, and fear of not living up to their magical goals. And since the confidence you have in your abilities as a magician (or witch) is hopelessly interconnected to your self-esteem, below you will find the complete recipe for making a talisman to carry with you whenever you lose faith in your divinatory talents.

Extra notes: it is advisable to perform the ritual on a Monday, Wednesday, or Friday or during the Moon's crescent phase.

Ingredients and magic items: a stone or crystal of your choice, an incense (of mint, chamomile, sage, or thyme). Remember to choose the one best suited to your needs depending on the season or day of the week you perform the ritual at your shrine. Then, also get a charcoal disc, matches, and a fireproof saucer (or tray).

Ritual: After purifying the altar, spread incense on the charcoal disk, burn it on the heat-proof saucer and close your eyes. Recite the formula: *"Along with the smoke, I dispel doubts and my low self-esteem."* Then, keep your eyes half-closed and consciously meditate on your intended goals (for about 5 minutes). Finally, open your eyes again and think back to the crystal, necklace, or piece of jewelry you chose for the ritual. Let it swing, back and forth, through the swirls of smoke emitted by the incense and repeat the chant, *"With each

step, I regenerate, shine and glow like the rays of the Sun" (for 3 times). Finally, take the talisman with you or leave it in your pocket. Remember to recharge it with beneficial vibrations every two months or so.

17 - *Healing amulet inspired by the Moon and its cycles*

Learn how to heal the *magical energies* within you with the help of the Moon! The amulet in question will enable you to increase your white (protective) power in a way that will keep evil eyes and dark curses away. I suggest you use a necklace made of *wood* and crystals. Otherwise, make use of a little wooden disc tied to a ribbon. The more experienced can make (or custom commission) an *iron* pendant.

Extra notes: perform the ritual during the full Moon phase.

Ingredients and magic items: a wooden chain or pendant, a few drops of eucalyptus essential oil, some matches, and a blue (or white) candle.

Ritual: After purifying the altar and workspace of your witchcraft workshop, sprinkle the candle with two drops of essential oil. Remember not to grease the wick to avoid unpleasant backfires. Next, light the votive candle and focus on the protective and healing energies contained within. Let the wooden necklace swing between the swirls of smoke emitted by the candle and repeat the formula: "*O my amulet, I infuse you with protective light and fill you with the energy of the full Moon. Protect me from every disease of the Earth.*"

Clasp the necklace between your fingers and visualize with your mind's eye the purifying vibrations melting into the palm of your hand. Then, blow out the candle and leave the pendant exposed on the windowsill for a whole night so that it becomes imbued with moonlight. Finally, wear the talisman as often as you feel the need to increase your strength. Remember to recharge it for one night during each Full Moon on the lunar calendar.

18 - *Friendship talisman*

From time to time, friendship relationships weaken, the affection we have for our acquaintances fades, and the feeling of brotherhood cools. To strengthen the bond with those closest to you, proceed with the making of the friendship talisman.

Extra note: I recommend that you perform the ritual on Sunday or during the New Moon phase.

Ingredients and magic items: five or six previously dried lavender flowers, a shard of crystal (preferably lapis lazuli), a miniature transparent flask, a string or chain about 45 centimeters long, and a piece of paper about 3 centimeters in size.

Ritual: Begin by purifying your altar. Then, draw on the slip of paper a *woven symbol that holds* the meaning of the friendship that binds you to the recipient of the spell. Roll or fold it so that it fits into the miniature flask, reciting aloud the formula: *"With this gesture, I regenerate our bond."* I suggest you focus on the face of your interlocutor in such a way as to call to you the memory of the positive energies shared with him/her. Then, add lavender sprouts

and recite the mantra, *"With the lavender of friendship, I bring back harmony and complicity."* Repeat the energetic process with lapis lazuli: *"With crystals, I infuse calm and courage, strength and energy."* Finally, take the necklace with you as a pendant or talisman to always have in your pocket. You could also make a second amulet for the friend or friend in question.

19 - Amulet to increase chances of a promotion at work

Staying chained to your desk in an unfulfilling office that prevents you from expressing your creative and imaginative verve is likely to turn into slavery that is difficult to tolerate. And so, I suggest you make a piece of good luck jewelry to place under your pillow before bed in order to understand *how, when, and why to* make the leap forward in your career.

Extra notes: proceed with the ritual on Thursday or Sunday or when the Moon is full or new.

Ingredients and magic items: two squares of fabric or felt (about 12 centimeters in size on each side), 5 ml of dried lavender (one teaspoon), 15 ml of dried rosemary (one tablespoon), paper, pen, needle, and thread. Finally, some bamboo to make the stuffing for the amulet.

Ritual: After purifying the altar, take pen and paper and write down in black and white all your professional goals. Do you intend to increase your monthly salary? Or keep yourself at arm's length from a "toxic," productivity- and performance-oriented environment

at whatever cost? Then overlap the two pieces of cloth or felt and sew them together along the edge. Leave only one side open, pour the stuffing inside, and turn the talisman inside out so that the seam is hidden inside. Next, lay the *sheet of wishes* inside your small *bag* and add thyme and lavender in the quantities mentioned above. As you proceed with the final magical steps, stay focused on your goals. Finally, close the last hem to seal the contents of the amulet. Done? Deposit the talisman under your pillow. Before surrendering to the dream world, ask yourself, "*What can I do to deserve the job situation to which I so aspire?*" Be patient and stand by <u>the answer will present itself to you in your dreams</u>.

20 - *Talisman for making a good first impression*

Job interview coming up? Or maybe you have to meet your better half's relatives for the first time, and you're afraid of making a bad impression? Or, again, do you want to make a good impression at the meeting that will give you access to greater chances for success and earnings? Regardless of the occasion that challenges your self-esteem, go ahead and make an *ad hoc* talisman.

Extra notes: perform the ritual on Sunday or when the New Moon shines in the sky.

Ingredients and magic items: any jewelry - preferably made from *green* materials - 15 ml of dried rose petals (a soup spoon), 15 ml of dried lavender, 15 ml of orange peel, 15 ml of dried lemon balm, mortar, and pestle, some matches, a heat-proof fireproof dish

(especially if you perform the spell indoors, in your workshop), charcoal disk, a small glass jar with a lid, and a funnel for decanting the above-mentioned ingredients.

Ritual: After purifying the altar and the four walls of your magic and witchcraft workshop, add rose petals, orange peel, lavender, and lemon balm to the mortar. Pound the ingredients gently and focus on your intended goal. Then, using the funnel, transfer the concoction to the glass jar. Light the charcoal with the matches and take a pinch of the mixture (with a teaspoon) to let it burn on the glowing disk. Finally, clasp the chosen talisman in your hands and swing it through the coal's effluvia, repeating the formula: "*I bless this amulet to make a good first impression.*"

I recommend that you specify aloud what qualities you intend to convey (courage, honesty, reliability, transparency, charisma, leadership, and so on). Finally, wear the jewel during the job interview or meeting. From time to time, refill it with the *green* blend kept in the pantry.

-CHAPTER 6-
Spells of Forgiveness, Protection, and Reversal

*S*orcerers, experienced or novice, report! Protection and reversal spells are crucial components of your journey of magic discovery. Not only do they allow you to exercise **forgiveness in** order to restore cosmic energies, but they also enable you to achieve a state of inner **peace** and **well-being.** I remind you that protection and reversal spells proceed hand in hand since they fulfill the goal of ensuring serenity and happiness for the sorcerer who masters them in the correct manner.

Happy reading and good magic!

21 - Protective barrier made with salt

The ritual in question can be performed whenever you believe your *sacred-personal* space is invaded by dark and evil energies. *Prepare a supply of protective salt to eradicate evil spirits at lightning speed!*

Extra notes: perform the ritual on Saturday or when the Moon is full.

Ingredients and magic items: 300 grams of salt, 5 ml of dried basil (one teaspoon), 5 ml of dried cloves, 5 ml of finely ground cumin, 5 ml of black pepper to ensure your well-being and protection. Also, obtain 5 ml of ash from a spell you have previously performed and a 500 ml jar (with lid).

Ritual: After cleansing the altar of previously accumulated negative vibrations, fill the jar with salt and add basil, cumin, cloves, ashes, and black pepper. Repeat the formula out loud:

*"Basil to protect,
cloves to repel the evil eye,
Cumin to guard my energy,
pepper to shield enemies
And ashes to defend myself."*

Close the jar with the cap and *shake it for a* few moments to mix the ingredients. Then, pour the *salt & spice* concoction all around the perimeter of your home. Check that the mixture is still there and that it is not dispersed by the wind or removed by malevolent sorcerers. In case the salt line turns out to be broken, repeat the ritual and spread the mixture for a second time.

22 - Seal of protection and defense

Seals are among my favorite protective spells. On the one hand, they allow the magician's creativity to run free; on the other hand, they allow him or her to reiterate the ritual quickly and efficiently. All you have to do is dip I and fingers in a mixture of purified water or essential oils to draw the protective seal on the windows and mirrors of your home.

Extra note: The ritual should be performed on a Saturday or during the New Moon phase.

Ingredients and magic items: permanent marker, pen and paper, and a flat-surfaced rock.

Ritual: Focus on the goal you intend to achieve after purifying the altar. Make a paper with the word **PROTECT** written on it. Make dashes, dots, and straight or curved lines out of the word

PROTECT. Combining the decomposed elements again, make a figure enclosed in a circle, square, triangle, or cross using the same piece of paper. Draw all the micro-elements of the word, being careful not to forget a single one. Try various combinations until you are sure you have devised your very own personal protective seal. You can then draw it on the smooth-surfaced stone or dip your fingers in purified water to reproduce it on the glass in your abode.

23 - Protection Spell with Iron

Among the minerals and metals, you should add to your sorcerer's larder as soon as possible, iron plays a major role. It is indeed a vehicle of <u>universal protection, as it is</u> present in large quantities in the stars and the earth we tread daily. In the magical arts, it is mostly used in the form of horseshoes, nails, or hematite.

Extra notes: perform the ritual on a Saturday or when the Moon is new or in its crescent phase.

Ingredients and magic objects: four or five iron objects (crystals or nails, for example), a dried bay leaf, 5 ml of cinnamon (one teaspoon), 5 ml of salt, matches, a heatproof dish, mortar and pestle, and a charcoal disk.

Ritual: Purify the altar in the way that suits you best. Then, add bay leaf, cinnamon, and salt to the mortar to create your own incense. Light the charcoal on the fireproof dish and let it burn until it becomes glowing. Next, add a pinch of incense to the disc and purify the iron objects between the swirls of fragrant smoke. In

the meantime, remember to focus on your magic and witchcraft goals. Meditate for about ten minutes with your eyes closed, trying to awaken the psychic force within you. Then, bury iron objects charged with white energy in the garden or under the potting soil. In this way, you will respect cosmic laws and allow the mineral to become part of the Planet again.

24 - *Protective mist*

What I propose below is the ritual of an enchanted nebulizer activated by the regenerative power of water and the natural properties of essential oils.

Extra notes: on Saturdays or when the Moon is black.

Ingredients and magic items: 150 ml of distilled water (you can also use tap water after boiling it and letting it cool to room temperature), 4 drops of sage essential oil, 4 drops of lavender essential oil, 4 drops of cedar essential oil, and a spray bottle with a capacity of about 150 ml.

Ritual: After purifying the altar or kitchen countertop, pour water into the bottle equipped with a nebulizer and add the essential oils *drop by drop*. Close the bottle and shake it for a few moments with your eyes closed and your mind focused on achieving your protection goals. Then, open your eyes, squeeze the nebulizer between your fingers, and visualize the energy enveloping the magical object through contact with your hand. Shake the bottle before each use.

25 - *Psychic Defense Wall (Advanced Spell)*

Advanced spells do not require more experience but rather a higher amount of mental energy. Accordingly, go ahead and perform the protective barrier on a day when you feel you are strong, healthy, and focused on the ultimate goals you intend to achieve. The defensive wall allows you to create an instant screen that protects the sorcerer's psychic qualities from the onset of any evil spirits and/or dark magic spells.

Extra notes: the first ritual must be compulsorily performed at the altar in your workshop. Afterward, you can reactivate your defensive powers wherever you need them.

Ingredients and magic items: protective mist (see previous spell) and opaque quartz crystal (if available).

Ritual: After purifying the altar, spray your **protective mist**. Then, sit in a comfortable position, close your eyes, and concentrate on the flow of your breath. To receive an additional energy boost, clasp a lucky charm amulet, or an opaque quartz crystal, in your hands. Finally, bring the focus back to your inner strength, imagine expanding it as if in an explosion, and visualize the presence of a shield a few inches away from you; it envelops you completely and conveys a feeling of security and invincibility. Open your eyes and activate the shield the instant you feel you are in danger. Repeat the spell as often as you wish.

26 - Bottled Defense Spell

What I recommend you transcribe into your very own personal *Grimoire* is a long-lasting spell. You will be able to enhance it with the addition of herbs and protective essential oils.

Extra notes: perform the ritual on Tuesday or during the New Moon.

Ingredients and magic objects: three iron objects (such as nails or hematite crystals), 15 ml black pepper (one soup spoon), 15 ml cumin, 15 ml salt, 15 ml cinnamon. Also, add a jar with a lid, pen, and paper, a protective seal-such as a friendship seal-and a white or brown candle about 4 inches high. Get some matches or a lighter.

Ritual: After purifying the altar, pour cumin, black pepper, salt, and cinnamon into your jar. Focus on your goals of protection. Then, draw the seal in black ink and stick the paper in the jar, along with the iron objects. Close the lid, light the candle, and tilt it in such a way as to create a glowing wax flow between the jar and its lid. Then place the votive candle on the jar and allow it to burn slowly. It could stay lit all night if necessary - but be careful not to place it near potentially flammable objects. Then, leave the protective jar by the front door of your abode.

27 - Purification ritual with tarot cards

Divination cards channel energy that promotes *forgiveness*. Consequently, the spell in question helps you illuminate the smoothest path to overcome existential obstacles.

Extra notes: perform the ritual on Sunday or Monday or when the Moon is black or full.

Ingredients and items: any Tarot deck, a white candle, a wand (Athame), paper and pen, and a match.

Ritual: Purify the altar and light the candle, focusing on your intended goals and intentions. Then grasp the wand with your dominant hand and draw a *defensive circle* around yourself. To succeed, point the Athame at the ground and visualize a white energy enveloping you as if inside a bubble isolated from the negative vibrations outside. Next, ask yourself three questions: **A)** What do I need to overcome the obstacle in front of me? **B)** What is preventing me from moving forward? **C)** What is the destination to be reached? Finally, sit on the ground and shuffle the Tarot cards. Let your intuition guide you, and stop the instant your intuition invites you to "put down" the figures. Arrange the cards in a fan shape on the surface of the altar, face down. Then, close your eyes and choose three cards completely intuitively. Turn them over. The first of the three Tarot cards provide an answer to the first question, the second to the next question, and the third to the last. Jot down in your magic notebook the messages conveyed by the intangible energy of the Tarot and try to understand how *Universal Truth* can help you overcome the obstacles that prevent you from proceeding courageously along the path that leads to happiness. After concluding the Tarot meditation, deactivate the circle of protection with the help of the Athame Wand or the *Witch's Dagger*.

28 - Spell to bless a new automobile

The spell in question is among the most requested by my *patrons*; it allows one to protect an automobile or bless any means of transportation in such a way that *negative karmic energies* do not cause accidents to the driver and any passengers.

Extra notes: perform the ritual during the New Moon phase.

Ingredients and magic items: get a square of black fabric (with sides about 25 centimeters), 10 ml of dried mugwort (that is, two teaspoons), 10 ml of dried juniper, 10 ml of cayenne pepper, 10 ml of black salt, 10 ml of cinnamon. Also take from your pantry a smoky turquoise quartz, a black votive candle, pen and paper, and a protective seal. Get a piece of string.

Ritual: After purifying the altar in the manner most congenial to you, light the votive candle and focus on the goal. Place the cloth handkerchief on the altar and arrange the above-mentioned ingredients (in order: mugwort, juniper, black salt, cayenne pepper and cinnamon) in the center. Recite the propitiatory formula, *"Herbs of protection, grant me your blessing."* Take the turquoise in your hand and tune into its energy; then, lay it on the herb-filled cloth and utter the chant, *"Stone of defense, infuse your properties."* Next, trace your very own protective seal on a piece of paper (with black ink) and add it to the mixture. Repeat the phrase, *"Seal, offer me your protection."* Finally, close the fabric square like a small bag and tie it with string. Keep it in your car. Before you get behind the wheel, visualize with your mind's eye the white light permeating the passenger compartment. Say out loud, *"Defense spell, spread in*

this place; bless my car in every part." Repeat the spell once or twice a month.

29 - *Tapestry of Protection*

What I recommend you transcribe into your personal *Grimoire* is a *spell object* to hang in your room, office, or inside your magic and witchcraft workshop.

Extra notes: perform the ritual on the Sabbath or during the Crescent or New Moon phase.

Ingredients and magic items: six small bells, six small objects made of ferrous materials (nails, screws, bolts, or cutlery you no longer use), string (or wool) strictly black in color to absorb negative energies, scissors, and four twigs with an approximate length of 15 centimeters.

Ritual: After purifying the altar, cut the twine into micro-strings no longer than 30 centimeters. You will need about 30 or so segments. Then, arrange the little woods on the altar and place the pieces of wool on the surface (at the four corners of the diamond). Next, knot the little woods together in such a way as to make a square/rhombus, and add the previously purified bells and iron objects. Follow your instincts, and do not worry about following a logical or aesthetic order. Finally, learn the tapestry of protection to the wall of your home. The bells will emit their *gentle tinkle whenever* your spells are strong enough to repel the forces of evil.

30 - Oil of the Warrior Fool

The ointment I suggest in this magical recipe aims to awaken the Warrior or Warrioress resting within you. I recommend that you use the oil directly on your skin or anoint your magical clothing before and after performing a spell. If you know you have particularly sensitive skin, consider testing the benefits of the Warrior Sorcerer's ointment on only a limited area - such as the back of your hand, for example.

Extra notes: do it on a Thursday or when the Moon is in its rising phase.

Ingredients and magic items: 30 ml of carrier oil (two tablespoons), 2 drops of cedar essential oil, 2 drops of rosemary essential oil, 2 drops of geranium essential oil, and an amber glass bottle fitted with a stopper.

Ritual: After purifying the altar or kitchen space designated for practice, pour the carrier oil into the bottle and add the drops of essential oils in order (cedar, geranium, and rosemary). Say aloud the formula: *"With this oil, nothing and no one can ever hit or hurt me again."* Then squeeze the bottle in your hands and visualize the positive energy surrounding it. The ointment is ready: use it on the skin by applying gentle pressure, or employ it on candles and magical objects of all kinds.

-Chapter 7-

The Grimoire of Happiness, Well-being, and Success

My dear reader, my dear reader, it's time to fight to get the life you've always wanted--with the *help of protection and reversal magic!* Those transcribed in these pages are spells, talismans, and ointments that-while not smoothing out all the obstacles in your existence-provide you with the *lifeblood you* need to approach success. *One step at a time!*

Good luck and good practice!

31 - *The Mirror of Holistic Wellness*

Needless to deny: we hear more and more frequently about *inner well-being*. Yet, few know where to start in order to transform into the "*improved*" version of themselves. The following spell is the wild card you can use to mature happiness, determination, and health. Are you ready to cut the furthest goals and climb even the highest peaks?

Extra notes: perform the ritual in the New Moon phase.

Ingredients and magic items: a portable mirror (preferably a resealable model), matches, a white-colored candle, paper, and a pen.

Ritual: After purifying the altar and laboratory, open the small mirror and place it on the work table. Light the candle, place it over the mirror, and recite aloud the following formula: "*This candle, with its light, generates a sense of peace within me.*" I suggest you meditate for about fifteen minutes, observing your reflection through the flickering flame of the votive candle. Seek within yourself the balance you need to increase well-being and happiness. Finally,

if you wish, write your reflections on a piece of paper or on the pages of your magic notebook. Blow out the candle and repeat the meditation session whenever you feel the need.

32 - *The balm that activates joy and psychic strength*

Ointments are undoubtedly the stars of *grimoires* around the world (*basic & advanced*). The one I have transcribed below is a *balm of abundance* that ignites your ability to nurture joy, satisfaction, and courage toward your achievements and the magical powers held within you.

Extra notes: perform the ritual on Thursday or when the Moon is full or new. In addition, I recommend performing the spell in the kitchen.

Ingredients and magic items: 50 grams beeswax flakes, 50 ml almond oil, 50 ml virgin coconut oil, ½ tablespoon Vitamin E oil, a medium-sized bowl inside which to mix the ingredients, and 3 micro-containers made of metal. You can also use glass jars with a capacity of about 80 to 90 ml.

Ritual: After purifying your kitchen countertop, pour the coconut oil and beeswax into the bowl. Heat them on the stove or in the microwave in 30-second intervals. Then repeat the process, stirring the concoction until it is melted (but not boiling). Next, add the almond oil and Vitamin E oil, focusing on the abundance and proliferation you intend to bring to your life. Finally, stir carefully and repeat aloud the propitiatory formula, *"Abundance, come to*

me. Abundance, *manifest yourself in my life.*" After you have the mixture, pour it into glass or metal micro-containers and let it solidify.

33 - *The seal of charisma and success*

No matter what anyone says about it, success can ensure the right *sprint* to our daily routine, filling it with joy and satisfaction. And since sigils are an expertly balanced mixture of inner creativity and highly personalized magical practices, the spell I propose will undoubtedly tickle your imaginative verve.

Extra notes: on Sundays or when the Moon is in its crescent phase.

Ingredients and magic items: get two slips of paper and a pen with orange ink.

Ritual: Purify the altar and write down an affirmation that represents Success with a capital S at a given time in your life. What's an example? *"I'm a skilled, courageous, and capable magician/witch."* Then remove all vowels from the sentence. Put the consonants in order. Here's what you'll get: "SKLLDCRGSCPBLWTCH." Break each letter into its basic elements: dots and dashes. In the same sheet, transcribe them using an orange pen. Put them together so that you get a fixed geometric figure: a cross, circle, square, or triangle. Then, transcribe them on the same sheet, making use of the orange pen. Take ten to fifteen minutes to combine them together so that you get a fixed geometric figure: a cross, circle, square, or triangle first.

Congratulations! You have just invented your very own seal of success!

Finally, redraw the seal on the other sheet of paper and keep it with you at all times to ensure its protection in the short and long term.

34 - Making a mela-magic

Not all sorcerers know that apples have the power - no, not just to keep the doctor away, but (also) to ward off the negative influences and bad luck that seem to doggedly pursue us!

Curious to know more?

Extra notes: during the New Moon phase.

Ingredients and magic items: a green apple, 20 cloves (whole), 5 ml cinnamon (one teaspoon), 5 ml allspice, 5 ml nutmeg, 5 ml ginger, 5 ml iris root (optional), matches, a green-colored candle, a small but deep bowl and a skewer made of wood or metal.

Ritual: After purifying the altar, light the candle with matches and focus on the target. Then pierce the fruit with the tip of the skewer so that there are about 20 holes large and deep enough to hold the cloves. As you insert the clove into the apple, speak aloud all the areas of life in which you wish to ward off the evil eye and receive benefits and good fortune. Next, mix the cinnamon, nutmeg, allspice, and ginger (as well as the rhizome, if you have it) in a bowl. Place the pot on the previously purified altar, and every day for three weeks, let the apple roll around inside the concoction for about five minutes. Repeat the process in the morning or evening, focusing on the existential aspects in which you wish to be most fortunate. Keep the enchanted fruit on your altar until its natural decay.

35 - Success rune cookies

Yum. It's time to infuse a dash of magic into your tea, milk, or coffee snacks. What I am proposing is a *hunger-busting* recipe inspired by the aforementioned Seal of Success. Feeding yourself magical foods will increase your *chances of* achieving the personal satisfaction and fulfillment you need to gain more confidence in your divinatory practices.

Extra notes: prepare the recipe in the kitchen on Sunday or during the New Moon phase.

Ingredients and magic items: 300 grams of flour, 100 grams of sugar, 100 grams of butter, 2 eggs, 1 packet of baking powder, 1 packet of vanillin, a large bowl for mixing the ingredients, a baking pan, some baking paper, and a knife.

Ritual: Before dressing up as a *magical chef*, cleanse the countertop in the kitchen. Then, preheat the oven to 180 degrees and pour all the ingredients into the bowl. Mix and add a little water in case the mixture is lumpy and uneven. Cover the dough with a tea towel and let it rest for an hour or so in the refrigerator. Then, divide it into balls about 5-6 centimeters in diameter and crush them on the baking sheet with the palm of your hand or with the help of a rolling pin. With the tip of a knife, carve the rune symbol of Success. Alternatively, trace the simplified *Sowulo rune* [see image below]. Bake the cookies in the oven for about 10 minutes and let them cool. Finally, enjoy them with a steaming cup of coffee, tuning into the positive vibrations that lead to the fulfillment of your innermost desires.

36 - *Magic cover to ensure your protection and safety*

Before proceeding with the spell in question, devote a witchcraft session to making your very own *Seal of Protection*. The latter will allow you to transform a simple blanket into a purified magical object capable of wrapping you inside a cocoon of joy, protection, and happiness!

Extra notes: the ritual is performed on a Saturday or Sunday or during a full Moon.

Magical ingredients and items: a blanket that is especially close to your heart, a purple votive candle, a permanent marker, matches, and a Seal of Protection.

Ritual: Before leaving, remember to purify the altar and the spell blanket. Then, light the candle and recall events and/or feelings that can convey joy, serenity, and relaxation in the body and mind. Clasp the blanket in your hands, close your eyes, and say aloud the following propitiatory formula:

"I bless this blanket, conveying to it the strength and security of the Earth.
I bless this blanket,
Infusing it with the heat and light emitted by the burning Fire.

I bless this blanket,
Transmitting to her the breath of the Air.
I bless this blanket,
Infusing it with the vitality and regenerative purity of Water."

I suggest you do not interrupt your witchcraft session without first closing your eyes to immerse yourself in a <u>five-minute meditation</u> on the theme of *prosperity*. Then, trace the Seal of Protection on the fabric with your permanent marker or a small brush dipped in ink.

37 - Restart potion for all the times you feel the need to (re)start from scratch

We've all dreamed of it at one time or another: how wonderful would it be to have a reboot button by means of which to erase the traces of the past and start again with renewed... *motivational momentum?* The energy of the Cosmos and Nature can come to your aid, especially if you decide to add this *reset* potion into your personal *Grimoire*.

Extra notes: on any day, as long as the Moon is in the *new* phase.

Ingredients and magic items: 1 liter of distilled water (or boiled and cooled to room temperature), a heliotrope crystal, a cup, a glass jar with a lid, 15 ml of dried verbena (one tablespoon), and 15 ml of dried nettle.

Ritual: After purifying the kitchen or altar intended for the spell, pour the water inside the jar and add the nettle in equal parts, then the verbena. Close the jar and place the heliotrope crystal on the lid

to imbue the mixture with positive, regenerative influences. Next, close your eyes and focus on the *personal and interpersonal goals you* intend to achieve. Leave the potion on the windowsill overnight and, after straining, drink it in a cup to introject the power of the New Moon.

38 - *Reversal spell to send his bad intentions back to the sender (Advanced Spell)*

In previous chapters, I have reiterated over and over again what strategies you can use to eradicate negativity and send any evil vibes back to the sender *(with interest!)*. After you've familiarized yourself with the *evil eye-banishing* spells, try your hand at this advanced spell.

Extra note: Perform the ritual during the waning Moon phase.

Ingredients and magic items: 5 ml of dried St. John's Wort (St. John's Wort) (one teaspoon), 5 ml of black salt, a fireproof bowl, paper, and a pen.

Ritual: After purifying your altar and the four walls of the magic and witchcraft workshop, write down on paper the goal you intend to achieve. Fold the paper and lay it inside the bowl. Then, sprinkle it with chopped St. John's Wort and black salt. Light a match and throw it into the fireproof bowl so as to ignite the ingredients of the *reversal ritual*. Sprinkle ashes around the perimeter and threshold of your dwelling so that the negative vibrations remain trapped and isolated outside.

39 - Spell to soothe the burden of responsibility

Responsibility is synonymous with *maturity*. Yet, from time to time, commitments and promises made to ourselves and others risk keeping us crushed under a boulder that annihilates creativity and our readiness to face the roller coaster of existence with a smile on our faces. So, add one of my favorite spells to your personal *grimoire*.

Extra notes: perform the ritual one hour before sunset, preferably outdoors.

Magic ingredients and items: bring a pen and paper, a plaid or any picnic blanket, a pinch of salt, and the **10 sticks** belonging to the Tarot deck (in the **Rider-Waite** variant). In the event that you are not in possession of the original version, print out an illustration found on the Internet or in some book on magic and witchcraft.

Ritual: Before proceeding with the actual spell, find a quiet little place where you can focus and feel comfortable. You can spread out a plaid and pillow to relax and familiarize yourself with the

practice of *outdoor* witchcraft. Then, draw a circle of protection by dispersing the salt all around you. Alternatively, you can make use of your wand. While doing so, visualize the white light enveloping you as within a bubble insulated from surrounding negativity and evil influences. Next, place the 10-of-sticks card in front of you and stare at the image with intensity and concentration. Try to imprint it in your mind. Close your eyes and allow yourself to be lulled into a *state of trance* and *deep focus*.

Immerse yourself in the character of the Tarot: why do you insist on dragging your sticks with you? Are the latter really necessary? Does your fictional interlocutor even have a chance to facilitate the task he is called upon to perform? Think through all the possible alternatives. Next, reopen your eyes and "*come back to the here and now.*" Take pen and paper, and jot down the micro-actions and micro-changes you can think of to relinquish, relieve or share with others the responsibilities that crush you at any given time in your existence. Purify the air and continue to reflect on the conclusions you have come to.

40 - *Potion to attract present and future love vibrations*

My dear reader, my dear reader, we conclude our journey of discovery of the *must-have* protective spells in the *Grimoire of* a budding sorcerer with a love potion.

Mind you: the latter does not manipulate the partner's behavior but allows the magician to access the **divinatory vision** that predicts

the future (with or without the company of your better half--present or future).

Extra notes: perform the ritual on a Friday or during the New Moon phase.

Ingredients and magic items: 5 ml dried rose petals (one teaspoon), 5 ml dried chamomile, 3 ml dried mugwort, 3 ml dried lemongrass, saucepan, quartz citrine, strainer, and cup for drinking the infusion.

Ritual: After purifying the kitchen countertop, bring the water to a boil and remove the pot from the flame. Then, add rose petals, mugwort, lemongrass, and chamomile (one ingredient at a time) to its interior. Next, clasp the citrine quartz fragment in the palm of your dominant hand and repeat the magic formula aloud:

> "With these ingredients,
> I amplify and reveal what is hidden;
> With this potion,
> I show what the crystal has chosen to reveal to me."

Continue stirring the concoction slowly, letting the ingredients steep for at least ten minutes. Finally, pour the potion into your cup (previously purified) and drink the strained mixture through the strainer while clutching the *energy-laden* quartz crystal in your dominant hand.

Conclusions

My dear Witch, I take off the *sorceress hat* I wear on my head to bow before your perseverance and to extend my sincerest congratulations to you! I hope that our (editorial) journey of discovery of ancient and modern witchcraft has tickled your fancy, triggering on the *inner lever* that allows everyone-no one excluded-to access the magic stored in the depths of the heart and psyche.

To continue to delve deeper into the mysterious magical arts, remember to add to your workshop shelves *the Encyclopedia of Magical Plants*, written by Scott Cunningham, and *The Magic Book of Incenses, Oils and Infusions* (also by Scott Cunningham). They will come in handy during the long stages of apprenticeship when essential oils and incense - as well as crystals and natural elements - will be the apotheosis of confusion, doubt, and mystery for you.

Don't beat yourself up: with a little practice, you'll train your mnestic skills and understand *how, when, and why to* rely on plants - depending on the season and origin of each ingredient. To proceed at a brisk pace along the road to divination, remember to purchase a *Grimoire* to write, update and modify in accordance with the spells, talismans, ointments, and seals that will become "*the highlights*" of your wizard or witch repertoire.

For my part, I have done my best to provide you with an overview of magic, both in its theoretical variants *(the law of impression, the law of harvest, and the law of analogy) and* in its practical spells. I hope to have intrigued you and to have torn apart, a little at a time,

the thick blanket of skepticism that cloaks the magical arts from the Middle Ages to the present day.

If you found my handbook useful and enabled you to learn the basics of divination, please share it and recommend it to your *"wannabe witches"* friends to support my bold outreach project. Even spontaneous feedback on Amazon and all major digital bookstores will allow me to grow, improve *and - why* not - answer the most popular questions in an updated version of the manual you hold in your hands.

I thank you for sticking with me to the end, and I greet you with the words of Paulo Coelho, *who - you guessed it!* - falls into the ranks of my favorite novelists:

"No day is the same; each morning brings with it its own particular miracle, its own magical moment in which old universes are destroyed and new stars are created."

Hoping to have accompanied you on your very personal journey of *Regeneration* and *Purification*...

Love,

Avril le Roux

Printed in Great Britain
by Amazon